THE TWO SHALL BECOME ONE

52 Weeks of Divine Union, Love, and Spiritual Growth

NEW CREATION
PRESS

CLEVELAND ORVILLE MCLEISH MTS

To every couple who has wept, prayed, fought, forgiven, hoped, and held on. This is for you.

PREFACE

We did not set out to write a devotional. We set out to grow.

My wife and I have known seasons of laughter, closeness, and joy. But we have also walked through long nights—through sickness, exhaustion, financial strain, separation due to work, prayers that seemed to go unanswered, and the deep loneliness that can come when no one fully sees your pain but God.

In those seasons, we discovered something we hadn't learned in the easy times:

- ى There is a deeper well to draw from.
- ى There is a love stronger than us.
- ى There is a mystery at the center of marriage that has little to do with romance and everything to do with covenant, with Christ, and with learning to walk as one.

This devotional was born from our journey—and from the stories of couples we have known and watched as they wrestled through the beautiful and brutal together.

It is my prayer that these pages will become a companion for you. That they will meet you on ordinary days and dark days, in seasons of celebration and seasons of ache. That they will help you lift your eyes together—beyond the surface, beyond survival—into the mystical, spiritual, deeply real union God invites you to live.

And that as you journey through these 52 weeks, you will discover you are not alone in your marriage, in your struggle, or in your desire for God.

You are held. You are loved. You are called into something far more beautiful than you can yet imagine.

Welcome to the journey.

TABLE OF CONTENTS

INTRODUCTION

MARRIAGE IS A MYSTERY

Marriage is a covenant made in time, yet it carries eternal weight. It is an earthly relationship, yet it reflects a heavenly reality. Scripture dares to call it a "great mystery," pointing to the union between Christ and His church (see Ephesians 5:32).

For many couples, this mystery feels distant. Life piles up: busy schedules, financial pressures, parenting demands, sickness, disappointment, grief. The very relationship meant to offer companionship can become strained by silence, resentment, or exhaustion. And when trials come—and they do/will—couples can find themselves struggling with each other, and with God.

This devotional was created for couples who long for more. Marriage is more than surface-level survival, more than coexisting under one roof, and more than occasional prayer or religious routine.

This devotional was written for those who want to step into union with God and with each other.

Here, over the course of 52 weeks, you will be invited to walk through key themes that every marriage faces: healing, forgiveness, communication, intimacy, sickness, loss, joy, spiritual disciplines, mystical union, and legacy.

Each week offers:

- A theme to center on.
- Scriptures for meditation.
- Guided meditations to help you quiet your hearts and listen.
- Wisdom from Christian mystics who have walked deeply with God.
- A Word for the week—conversational, practical, theologically grounded.
- A Psalm to pray.
- Declarations to speak over your lives.
- A Communion moment to receive Christ's life together.
- A final word to carry into your days.

Along the way, you will practice spiritual disciplines, not as heavy obligations, but as ancient technologies God has given us to access the reality of His kingdom. Prayer, fasting, worship, silence, and communion are not just religious acts. They are portals into God's presence, and they carry real power to heal, restore, and transform.

As you engage in these practices together, you will not only strengthen your marriage but also open your lives to the Spirit of God, who alone can make you one.

This devotional is not about fixing everything overnight. It is about walking faithfully, one week at a time, into deeper love with God, with your spouse, and with yourself.

You are not alone on this journey. You are not left to human strength. The God who called you into union is the God who will sustain you in it.

Step in. He is waiting.

FOUNDATIONS

(union, healing, forgiveness, communication, love, faith)

WEEK 1
THE MYSTERY OF UNION—YOU ARE NOT ALONE

MEDITATION SCRIPTURES

"For we are members of His body, of His flesh and of His bones."
—Ephesians 5:30 (NKJV)

"And this is why a man leaves father and mother and cherishes his wife. No longer two, they become 'one flesh.' This is a huge mystery, and I don't pretend to understand it all. What is clearest to me is the way Christ treats the church. —Ephesians 5:31–32 (MSG)

"The person who is joined to the Lord is one spirit with Him." — 1 Corinthians 6:17 (NASB)

GUIDED MEDITATION ON SCRIPTURE

Sit together in stillness. Breathe slowly. Hold hands or place a hand on each other's shoulder.

Read the scriptures aloud three times, slowly, letting the words rest in the room.

Afterward, close your eyes and silently ask:

- ی What does it mean that we are "one flesh"?
- ی What does it mean to be "one spirit" with the Lord?

Notice any images, thoughts, or feelings that arise. Stay quiet together for a few minutes, just resting in God's presence.

QUOTE FOR TODAY

"The soul is made of love and must ever strive to return to love. Therefore, it can never find rest nor happiness in other things. It must lose itself in love."

— *Mechthild of Magdeburg*

WORD FOR THE WEEK

Marriage is not just a social contract; it is a living mystery. Scripture calls it a "great mystery," reflecting the mystical union between Christ and the church. When you and your spouse joined your lives, you entered something much deeper than a legal agreement—you entered a spiritual oneness.

This oneness means that in your joys and in your struggles, you are never alone. You carry one another's burdens, and together, you are joined to Christ. His strength flows into your weakness. His love fills the spaces where human love feels too small. When sickness, sorrow, or pressure overwhelm you, you are not left to face them with human effort alone. You are in covenant with the living God.

But this union is not automatic in experience; it is something we must consciously enter. Spiritual disciplines like prayer, worship, and communion are not religious duties. They are technologies of union, ways we enter and participate in the life of God. When you pray, you are not just asking for things; you are sharing heart-to-heart with the One who dwells in you. When you worship, you join the song of heaven that sustains the cosmos.

This week, remember: you and your spouse are not just partners; you are one body, joined to Christ. Let this mystery shape how you speak, how you love, how you carry burdens, and how you pray. Draw near to God and to each other and you will find resources that far exceed your own.

PSALM TO MEDITATE ON

"God is our refuge and strength, a very present help in trouble. Therefore we will not fear, even though the earth be removed, and though the mountains be carried into the midst of the sea." — Psalm 46:1–2 (NKJV)

GUIDED MEDITATION ON THE PSALM

Read the psalm aloud slowly. Picture the mountains shaking, the sea roaring, yet God remains your unshakable refuge.

Together, ask:

- Where do we need God's refuge right now?
- Where have we tried to carry things alone?

Take turns naming those areas aloud. Then, in silence, imagine placing those burdens at God's feet.

DECLARATIONS FOR THE WEEK

We declare:

- ﭺ We are one flesh in Christ, joined by His love and Spirit.
- ﭺ God is our refuge and strength in every storm.
- ﭺ Our marriage is upheld by God's supernatural grace.
- ﭺ We release past wounds and receive fresh unity and joy.
- ﭺ We are not alone—heaven's help is with us.

COMMUNION: RECEIVING CHRIST'S LIFE INTO OUR MARRIAGE

Communion is more than a ritual; it is a living encounter. When we eat the bread, we receive the healing, wholeness, and resurrection life of Jesus. When we drink the cup, we enter His covenant of forgiveness, love, and victory.

Jesus said, **"This is My body, given for you"** (see Luke 22:19). His body carries your sickness, your sorrow, your brokenness, and gives you His strength. His blood speaks a better word over you: forgiveness, reconciliation, and a future filled with hope.

COMMUNION PRAYER

(Prepare bread (or a cracker) and a small cup of juice. Together, hold the bread and pray).

Lord Jesus Christ, we come before You now, humbled and grateful. You are the Bread of Life, the true Manna from heaven. You gave Your body to be broken for us, that we might be made whole—spirit, soul, and body. You poured out Your blood as the cup of the new covenant, that we might be cleansed, forgiven, and reconciled to God.

We pause to remember Your sacrifice. We remember Your wounds, Your love, Your victory. We remember that You carried our sickness, our grief, our sins, and our shame upon Yourself at the cross (see Isaiah 53:4–5). You conquered death, hell, and the grave, and You rose again, so that we might share in Your life.

We confess, Lord, that we need You. We bring before You every place in our lives and marriage where we are weak, divided, hurting, or burdened. We ask for Your forgiveness for where we have spoken in anger, withheld love, carried resentment, or failed to honor one another. Wash us clean, Jesus—in Your mercy, cover us with Your righteousness.

As we eat this bread, we receive Your healing. Heal our hearts where they are wounded. Heal our minds where they are anxious or tormented. Heal our bodies where they are sick or weak. Heal our marriage where it has been strained or broken. Let the same power that raised You from the dead now flow through us. Jesus, thank You for giving Your body for us. We receive Your healing and wholeness today.

(Eat the bread)

As we drink this cup, we renew our covenant with You and with each other. We declare that we are Yours, and You are ours. We belong to You—as individuals and as a couple. Strengthen the bond between us. Let our love be patient, kind, humble, and enduring. Let forgiveness flow freely in our home. Let Your peace reign over our household. Jesus, thank You for Your blood, poured out in love. We receive Your forgiveness, Your protection, and Your life.

(Drink the cup)

Jesus, fill us with Your Spirit. Unite us in Your love. Draw us deeper into the mystery of union with You—that we may be one as You and the Father are one. Teach us to love one another with Your supernatural love. Teach us to walk in Your ways. Teach us to see our marriage not only as partnership, but as a holy vessel that carries Your glory into this world.

We receive now—with faith and joy—the blessings You have promised. Blessings of peace, healing, provision, restoration, protection, wisdom, and overflowing grace. We stand in agreement, as one, declaring that no weapon formed against us shall prosper. We break every assignment of the enemy against our lives and marriage. We release blessing over our future, over our family, and over the generations to come.

Thank You, Jesus, for Your body and blood, given freely for us. We honor You, we love You, and we give You all the glory. In Your holy name we pray. Amen.

AFTER-COMMUNION DECLARATIONS

- ﺷ Our marriage is strengthened by His love.
- ﺷ We walk in covenant blessing and divine protection.
- ﺷ We are one—with God, and with each other.
- ﺷ We speak healing over our minds, bodies, and marriage.
- ﺷ We are healed and made whole through Christ.
- ﺷ We declare peace over our home.
- ﺷ We receive divine strength to carry every burden with hope.
- ﺷ We stand in covenant with You, Jesus, and with one another.

FINAL WORD

This week, practice stepping into the mystery. Speak kindly. Pray intentionally. Laugh together. Carry one another with tenderness. And when you stumble, remember: grace is the ground beneath your feet.

CLOSING PRAYER

"Jesus, unite us in Your love. Fill our marriage with Your presence. Let our home be a place where heaven and earth meet. Amen."

WEEK 2
HEALING IN THE HIDDEN PLACES— LETTING GOD TOUCH WHAT WE CANNOT FIX

MEDITATION SCRIPTURES

"He heals the brokenhearted and binds up their wounds."—Psalm 147:3 (NKJV)

"He heals the heartbroken and bandages their wounds."—Psalm 147:3 (MSG)

"Come to Me, all who are weary and burdened, and I will give you rest. Take My yoke upon you and learn from Me, for I am gentle and humble in heart, and you will find rest for your souls."— Matthew 11:28–29 (NASB)

GUIDED MEDITATION ON SCRIPTURE

Sit together quietly. Take a few deep breaths. Imagine yourselves sitting at the feet of Jesus.

Read the scriptures aloud slowly, two or three times. Then ask inwardly:

ى What wounds in my heart still need His healing?

ﻉ   What burden am I carrying that feels too heavy?

ﻉ   Where do I long for my marriage to experience rest?

Stay in the silence together, letting the Spirit show you gently. You do not need to fix anything right now. Just listen.

QUOTE FOR TODAY

"God alone can fill the soul; it is only with God that the soul can find peace and rest."

—*St. John of the Cross*

WORD FOR THE WEEK

Marriage brings great joy, but it also uncovers deep wounds—some we did not even know were there. Often, couples discover that the stress and conflict they face together are not just about money, sickness, or time, but about the hidden places in their hearts that have not yet been healed.

There may be grief you never fully processed. There may be guilt over past choices, or shame that you carry silently. There may be anger you've buried so long you no longer recognize it as anger. And sometimes, the one you love most is the mirror God uses to show you where you are hurting.

Jesus does not stand at a distance, demanding you fix yourself. He comes close to touch, to tend, to heal. When you let Him into the hidden places, you allow His love to transform what you cannot change by willpower. This is true not only for you as individuals, but for your marriage. Healing happens when you both turn toward Him together, in your weakness, and invite Him to work.

This week, open your hearts in a fresh way. You do not need to perform for God, and you do not need to perform for each other. Come honestly. Come quietly. Let His love begin to soften the hard places, mend the broken places, and bring rest to your weary souls.

PSALM TO MEDITATE ON

"Search me, O God, and know my heart; try me, and know my anxieties; and see if there is any wicked way in me, and lead me in the way everlasting."—Psalm 139:23–24 (NKJV)

GUIDED MEDITATION ON THE PSALM

Read the psalm aloud. Then sit in quiet.

Together or silently, ask:

- ی Lord, search us.
- ی What are You lovingly bringing to the surface?
- ی Where are You inviting us to let go, so You can heal?

Picture God's light gently shining into your hearts, not to accuse, but to heal and lead you into freedom.

DECLARATIONS FOR THE WEEK

We declare:

- We are safe in God's love to be honest and whole.
- Jesus is healing every hidden wound and lifting every burden.
- Our marriage is being restored by His kindness and grace.
- We welcome the Holy Spirit to search us and lead us.
- We receive rest for our souls and peace for our home.

COMMUNION PRAYER

(Prepare bread (or a cracker) and a small cup of juice. Together, hold the bread and pray).

Lord Jesus Christ, we come before You now, humbled and grateful. You are the Bread of Life, the true Manna from heaven. You gave Your body to be broken for us, that we might be made whole—spirit, soul, and body. You poured out Your blood as the cup of the new covenant, that we might be cleansed, forgiven, and reconciled to God.

We pause to remember Your sacrifice. We remember Your wounds, Your love, Your victory. We remember that You carried our sickness, our grief, our sins, and our shame upon Yourself at the cross (see Isaiah 53:4–5). You conquered death, hell, and the grave, and You rose again, so that we might share in Your life.

We confess, Lord, that we need You. We bring before You every place in our lives and marriage where we are weak, divided, hurting, or

burdened. We ask for Your forgiveness for where we have spoken in anger, withheld love, carried resentment, or failed to honor one another. Wash us clean, Jesus—in Your mercy, cover us with Your righteousness.

As we eat this bread, we receive Your healing. Heal our hearts where they are wounded. Heal our minds where they are anxious or tormented. Heal our bodies where they are sick or weak. Heal our marriage where it has been strained or broken. Let the same power that raised You from the dead now flow through us. Jesus, thank You for Your body, broken for our healing. As we eat this bread, we receive wholeness in our bodies, in our minds, in our emotions, and in our marriage.

(Eat the bread)

As we drink this cup, we renew our covenant with You and with each other. We declare that we are Yours, and You are ours. We belong to You—as individuals and as a couple. Strengthen the bond between us. Let our love be patient, kind, humble, and enduring. Let forgiveness flow freely in our home. Let Your peace reign over our household. Jesus, thank You for Your blood, poured out for forgiveness and new life. As we drink this cup, we receive mercy, restoration, and the victory of Your resurrection.

(Drink the cup)

Jesus, fill us with Your Spirit. Unite us in Your love. Draw us deeper into the mystery of union with You—that we may be one as You and

the Father are one. Teach us to love one another with Your supernatural love. Teach us to walk in Your ways. Teach us to see our marriage not only as partnership, but as a holy vessel that carries Your glory into this world.

We receive now—with faith and joy—the blessings You have promised. Blessings of peace, healing, provision, restoration, protection, wisdom, and overflowing grace. We stand in agreement, as one, declaring that no weapon formed against us shall prosper. We break every assignment of the enemy against our lives and marriage. We release blessing over our future, over our family, and over the generations to come.

Thank You, Jesus, for Your body and blood, given freely for us. We honor You, we love You, and we give You all the glory. In Your holy name we pray. Amen.

AFTER-COMMUNION DECLARATIONS

- ی We speak healing over every part of our lives.
- ی We declare freedom over past pain, mistakes, and shame.
- ی We bless our marriage with unity, tenderness, and peace.

Jesus, make us whole—in You, together. Amen.

FINAL WORD

This week, trust the slow and tender work of God. Healing rarely happens in a rush. But when you make space, when you bring your hearts to Him honestly, He will always meet you. And what He touches, He makes whole.

WEEK 3
THE POWER OF FORGIVENESS—
LETTING GO TO HOLD ON

MEDITATION SCRIPTURES

"Be kind to one another, tenderhearted, forgiving one another, even as God in Christ forgave you."—Ephesians 4:32 (NKJV)

"Make allowances for each other's faults, and forgive anyone who offends you. Remember, the Lord forgave you, so you must forgive others."—Colossians 3:13 (NLT)

"Above all, love each other deeply, because love covers over a multitude of sins."—1 Peter 4:8 (NASB)

GUIDED MEDITATION ON SCRIPTURE

Sit quietly together. Hold hands or place a hand over each other's heart.

Read the scriptures slowly, pausing after each. Breathe deeply. Ask silently:

> ∽ Where have I held on to offense, resentment, or disappointment?

ی Where do I need to release forgiveness—toward my spouse, myself, or even God?

Stay in stillness for a few moments, letting God's gentle light reveal what needs to be healed and released.

QUOTE FOR TODAY

"The soul that loves God finds peace in everything, and is troubled by nothing, for it rests in the perfect embrace of forgiveness."
—*Catherine of Siena*

WORD FOR THE WEEK

Forgiveness is not an occasional act—it is the atmosphere of a thriving marriage. Two imperfect people living in covenant will, without doubt, hurt, fail, and disappoint each other at times. But forgiveness is the holy glue that holds them together, even when the cracks appear.

Forgiveness does not mean pretending nothing happened. It means acknowledging the pain, bringing it before God, and choosing to release your spouse from the debt of "you owe me." It means trusting that God, who forgave us completely, will empower us to forgive— again and again, as many times as needed.

Some wounds are light; they heal quickly. Others go deep and need time, tears, and help to mend. But forgiveness is always the first step toward healing. It opens the door to reconciliation, intimacy, and peace. Without it, even the smallest offenses can build a wall between hearts.

This week, choose to be courageous forgivers. Whether you need to forgive your spouse, yourself, or even God (where you have felt disappointed or abandoned), bring it all into His presence. Forgiveness frees you to love fully again. It frees your home to be a sanctuary of grace.

PSALM TO MEDITATE ON

"Have mercy upon me, O God, according to Your lovingkindness; according to the multitude of Your tender mercies, blot out my transgressions… Create in me a clean heart, O God, and renew a steadfast spirit within me."—Psalm 51:1, 10 (NKJV)

GUIDED MEDITATION ON THE PSALM

Read Psalm 51 slowly. Let it become your prayer.

Ask:

- ﺱ Lord, where do I need Your mercy today?
- ﺱ Where do we, as a couple, need a fresh start?

Picture God washing over you both with mercy, cleansing old wounds, renewing love, and restoring joy.

DECLARATIONS FOR THE WEEK

We declare:

- ي We are a forgiving and forgiven couple.
- ي God's mercy is greater than our failures.
- ي We release every hurt, offense, and disappointment into His hands.
- ي Our marriage is covered by grace and strengthened by love.
- ي We walk in freedom, peace, and renewed intimacy.

COMMUNION PRAYER

(Prepare bread (or a cracker) and a small cup of juice. Together, hold the bread and pray).

Lord Jesus Christ, we come before You now, humbled and grateful. You are the Bread of Life, the true Manna from heaven. You gave Your body to be broken for us, that we might be made whole—spirit, soul, and body. You poured out Your blood as the cup of the new covenant, that we might be cleansed, forgiven, and reconciled to God.

We pause to remember Your sacrifice. We remember Your wounds, Your love, Your victory. We remember that You carried our sickness, our grief, our sins, and our shame upon Yourself at the cross (see Isaiah 53:4–5). You conquered death, hell, and the grave, and You rose again, so that we might share in Your life.

We confess, Lord, that we need You. We bring before You every place in our lives and marriage where we are weak, divided, hurting, or

burdened. We ask for Your forgiveness for where we have spoken in anger, withheld love, carried resentment, or failed to honor one another. Wash us clean, Jesus—in Your mercy, cover us with Your righteousness.

As we eat this bread, we receive Your healing. Heal our hearts where they are wounded. Heal our minds where they are anxious or tormented. Heal our bodies where they are sick or weak. Heal our marriage where it has been strained or broken. Let the same power that raised You from the dead now flow through us. Jesus, thank You that You have forgiven us—fully, freely, forever. As we eat this bread, we remember Your body broken for our healing, including the healing of our hearts and marriage.

(Eat the bread)

As we drink this cup, we renew our covenant with You and with each other. We declare that we are Yours, and You are ours. We belong to You—as individuals and as a couple. Strengthen the bond between us. Let our love be patient, kind, humble, and enduring. Let forgiveness flow freely in our home. Let Your peace reign over our household. Jesus, thank You for Your blood, poured out for forgiveness and new life. As we drink this cup, we remember Your blood shed for our forgiveness. We stand in Your mercy, releasing one another from the debts of the past.

(Drink the cup)

Jesus, fill us with Your Spirit. Unite us in Your love. Draw us deeper into the mystery of union with You—that we may be one as You and the Father are one. Teach us to love one another with Your supernatural love. Teach us to walk in Your ways. Teach us to see our marriage not only as partnership, but as a holy vessel that carries Your glory into this world.

We receive now—with faith and joy—the blessings You have promised. Blessings of peace, healing, provision, restoration, protection, wisdom, and overflowing grace. We stand in agreement, as one, declaring that no weapon formed against us shall prosper. We break every assignment of the enemy against our lives and marriage. We release blessings over our future, over our family, and over the generations to come.

Thank You, Jesus, for Your body and blood, given freely for us. We honor You, we love You, and we give You all the glory. In Your holy name we pray. Amen.

AFTER COMMUNION DECLARATIONS

- ৬ May we love with Your patience.
- ৬ May we forgive as You forgive.
- ৬ May our marriage reflect Your redeeming grace.
- ৬ Jesus, make us one again. Amen.

FINAL WORD

Forgiveness is not weakness—it is fierce love. It is the love that God has shown you, now made visible between you. Let go of what weighs you down, so you can hold on to each other in freedom, joy, and peace.

WEEK 4
GRACE FOR TODAY—LIVING WITH WEAKNESS AND STRENGTH

MEDITATION SCRIPTURES

"But He said to me, 'My grace is sufficient for you, for My strength is made perfect in weakness.' Therefore most gladly I will rather boast in my infirmities, that the power of Christ may rest upon me."—2 Corinthians 12:9 (NKJV)

"Each time He said, 'My grace is all you need. My power works best in weakness.' So now I am glad to boast about my weaknesses, so that the power of Christ can work through me."—2 Corinthians 12:9 (NLT)

"For we do not have a high priest who cannot sympathize with our weaknesses, but One who has been tempted in all things just as we are, yet without sin. Therefore, let's approach the throne of grace with confidence, so that we may receive mercy and find grace for help at the time of our need."—Hebrews 4:15–16 (NASB)

GUIDED MEDITATION ON SCRIPTURE

Sit quietly together. Close your eyes and breathe slowly.

Read the scriptures aloud. Let the words wash over you: **"My grace is sufficient... My power works best in weakness... Receive mercy... find grace for help."**

Ask silently:

- ☞ Where am I feeling weak right now?
- ☞ Where is my spouse feeling weak?
- ☞ Where do we need to stop striving and simply receive God's grace?

Spend a few moments in stillness, letting God's presence rest on you both.

QUOTE FOR TODAY

"All the way to heaven is heaven, because Jesus said, 'I am the way.'"
—*Catherine of Siena*

WORD FOR THE WEEK

Marriage invites us into a truth we often resist: we are not as strong as we think. We cannot carry every burden, fix every problem, meet every need, or be everything to one another. And yet, somehow, we are called to walk this road together—weak, limited, human.

This is not failure; this is design. Scripture tells us that God's strength is made perfect in our weakness. His power is not revealed through our performance but through our surrender. When we bring our need to Him—individually and as a couple—we make room for Him to do what we cannot.

Grace is not just the forgiveness of sins; it is the empowering presence of God in the places where we are lacking. Grace carries you through sleepless nights, hospital rooms, financial pressures, difficult conversations, and seasons where your own strength runs out. Grace means that you do not walk alone and that God will supply what you need, one day at a time.

This week, resist the pressure to "have it all together." Instead, come humbly before God and each other. Admit where you are tired, scared, or worn thin. Then lift your eyes and let the grace of God cover you both, like fresh rain on dry ground.

PSALM TO MEDITATE ON

"I will lift up my eyes to the hills— from whence comes my help? My help comes from the Lord, who made heaven and earth."— Psalm 121:1–2 (NKJV)

GUIDED MEDITATION ON THE PSALM

Read Psalm 121 aloud slowly.

Imagine lifting your eyes to the hills. See God, your Helper, coming toward you.

Ask together:

- ی Where do we need help this week?
- ی Where can we stop depending on ourselves and turn to Him?

Picture yourselves laying down every burden at His feet and receiving help from His hand.

DECLARATIONS FOR THE WEEK

We declare:

- ی God's grace is sufficient for us today.
- ی His power is made perfect in our weakness.
- ی We will no longer strive or carry burdens alone.
- ی We lift our eyes to the Lord, our ever-present help.
- ی We receive fresh strength, fresh mercy, fresh grace.

COMMUNION PRAYER

(Prepare bread (or a cracker) and a small cup of juice. Together, hold the bread and pray).

Lord Jesus Christ, we come before You now, humbled and grateful. You are the Bread of Life, the true Manna from heaven. You gave Your body to be broken for us, that we might be made whole—spirit, soul, and body. You poured out Your blood as the cup of the new covenant, that we might be cleansed, forgiven, and reconciled to God.

We pause to remember Your sacrifice. We remember Your wounds, Your love, Your victory. We remember that You carried our sickness, our grief, our sins, and our shame upon Yourself at the cross (see Isaiah 53:4–5). You conquered death, hell, and the grave, and You rose again, so that we might share in Your life.

We confess, Lord, that we need You. We bring before You every place in our lives and marriage where we are weak, divided, hurting, or burdened. We ask for Your forgiveness for where we have spoken in anger, withheld love, carried resentment, or failed to honor one another. Wash us clean, Jesus—in Your mercy, cover us with Your righteousness.

As we eat this bread, we receive Your healing. Heal our hearts where they are wounded. Heal our minds where they are anxious or tormented. Heal our bodies where they are sick or weak. Heal our marriage where it has been strained or broken. Let the same power that raised You from the dead now flow through us. Jesus, we come to You weary and in need. As we eat this bread, we receive Your body—broken so we could be made whole.

(Eat the bread)

As we drink this cup, we renew our covenant with You and with each other. We declare that we are Yours, and You are ours. We belong to You—as individuals and as a couple. Strengthen the bond between us. Let our love be patient, kind, humble, and enduring. Let forgiveness flow freely in our home. Let Your peace reign over our household. Jesus, thank You for Your blood, poured out for forgiveness and new life. As we drink this cup, we remember Your blood shed for our forgiveness. We lay down our striving. We confess that we cannot do this in our own strength. We open our hands to receive Your grace—to sustain our hearts, our marriage, our family, and our future. Pour Your Spirit into us. Fill what is empty. Strengthen what is weak. Make our home a place where Your power is seen, not because we are perfect, but because we belong to You. As we drink this cup, we receive Your blood—poured out to cover every failure and supply every need.

(Drink the cup)

Jesus, fill us with Your Spirit. Unite us in Your love. Draw us deeper into the mystery of union with You—that we may be one as You and the Father are one. Teach us to love one another with Your supernatural love. Teach us to walk in Your ways. Teach us to see our marriage not only as partnership, but as a holy vessel that carries Your glory into this world.

We receive now—with faith and joy—the blessings You have promised. Blessings of peace, healing, provision, restoration, protection, wisdom, and overflowing grace. We stand in agreement, as one, declaring that no weapon formed against us shall prosper. We break every assignment of the enemy against our lives and marriage. We release blessings over our future, over our family, and over the generations to come.

Thank You, Jesus, for Your body and blood, given freely for us. We honor You, we love You, and we give You all the glory. In Your holy name we pray. Amen.

FINAL WORD

You are not asked to be perfect this week—only to be present, honest, and open. His grace will meet you where you are, not where you think you should be. And in that grace, you will find strength to carry on, together.

WEEK 5
SACRED COMMUNICATION—SPEAKING WITH LOVE AND LISTENING WITH HEART

MEDITATION SCRIPTURES

"Let no corrupt word proceed out of your mouth, but what is good for necessary edification, that it may impart grace to the hearers."— Ephesians 4:29 (NKJV)

"Everyone should be quick to listen, slow to speak, and slow to become angry, for human anger does not produce the righteousness that God desires."—James 1:19–20 (NIV)

"The right word at the right time is like a custom-made piece of jewelry, and a wise friend's timely reprimand is like a gold ring slipped on your finger."—Proverbs 25:11–12 (MSG)

GUIDED MEDITATION ON SCRIPTURE

Sit together in quiet. Take a few deep breaths and relax.

Read the scriptures slowly, pausing after each. Reflect silently:

ى When have my words brought grace—or harm—to my spouse?

ی   Where do I need to listen better, speak more gently, or slow down?

Sit in silence for a few moments, asking God to help you notice the patterns in your communication—and inviting Him to guide your conversations this week.

QUOTE FOR TODAY

"Where there is charity and wisdom, there is neither fear nor ignorance. Where there is patience and humility, there is neither anger nor disturbance."

—*St. Francis of Assisi*

WORD FOR THE WEEK

Words shape the atmosphere of a marriage. With them, we can build a home of peace, tenderness, and connection—or one of tension, frustration, and distance. What we speak (and how we listen) carries spiritual weight. Words are not just sounds; they are seeds that grow into the culture of your relationship.

Many couples fall into predictable patterns: one speaks quickly, while the other withdraws; one raises their voice, while the other shuts down; one dominates, while the other resents. Left unexamined, these patterns can choke intimacy. But God invites us to practice a different kind of communication—one shaped by love, humility, and patience.

Good communication is not just about solving problems or avoiding conflict. It is about learning to hear your spouse's heart, not just their words. It is about asking, *"What are they really longing for? What fear or hope is underneath this conversation?"* It is about letting the Holy Spirit soften your responses, giving you wisdom to speak life instead of adding fuel to the fire.

This week, take time to listen—not to fix, but to understand. Speak—not to win, but to bless. Ask God to help you slow down, hold space, and honor each other with your words. Every conversation can become holy ground.

PSALM TO MEDITATE ON

"Set a guard, O Lord, over my mouth; keep watch over the door of my lips."—Psalm 141:3 (NKJV)

GUIDED MEDITATION ON THE PSALM

Read Psalm 141 aloud. Pause and picture God gently guarding your words.

Ask together:

- Lord, where do we need Your help with our speech?
- How can we create more room to listen well this week?

Sit quietly for a moment, asking God to reveal one small change you can make in how you speak or listen.

DECLARATIONS FOR THE WEEK

We declare:

- ى Our words will bring grace, healing, and life to one another.
- ى We will be quick to listen, slow to speak, and slow to anger.
- ى The Holy Spirit is teaching us to understand each other deeply.
- ى Our conversations are becoming holy and fruitful.
- ى We are creating a home filled with love, wisdom, and peace.

COMMUNION PRAYER

(Prepare bread (or a cracker) and a small cup of juice. Together, hold the bread and pray).

Lord Jesus Christ, we come before You now, humbled and grateful. You are the Bread of Life, the true Manna from heaven. You gave Your body to be broken for us, that we might be made whole—spirit, soul, and body. You poured out Your blood as the cup of the new covenant, that we might be cleansed, forgiven, and reconciled to God.

We pause to remember Your sacrifice. We remember Your wounds, Your love, Your victory. We remember that You carried our sickness, our grief, our sins, and our shame upon Yourself at the cross (see Isaiah 53:4–5). You conquered death, hell, and the grave, and You rose again, so that we might share in Your life.

We confess, Lord, that we need You. We bring before You every place in our lives and marriage where we are weak, divided, hurting, or burdened. We ask for Your forgiveness for where we have spoken in anger, withheld love, carried resentment, or failed to honor one another. Wash us clean, Jesus—in Your mercy, cover us with Your righteousness.

As we eat this bread, we receive Your healing. Heal our hearts where they are wounded. Heal our minds where they are anxious or tormented. Heal our bodies where they are sick or weak. Heal our marriage where it has been strained or broken. Let the same power that raised You from the dead now flow through us. Jesus, thank You that You are the Living Word, full of grace and truth. As we eat this bread, we remember that You gave Your body for us—to heal not just our wounds, but also the wounds we inflict with our words.

(Eat the bread)

As we drink this cup, we renew our covenant with You and with each other. We declare that we are Yours, and You are ours. We belong to You—as individuals and as a couple. Strengthen the bond between us. Let our love be patient, kind, humble, and enduring. Let forgiveness flow freely in our home. Let Your peace reign over our household. Jesus, thank You for Your blood, poured out for forgiveness and new life. As we drink this cup, we receive Your forgiveness and the power to forgive each other. We invite You into our conversations, our conflicts, and our silences. Fill our mouths with wisdom. Fill our hearts with understanding. Let our communication become a reflection of Your love, not our

48

frustrations. Thank You, Lord, that You speak peace over our marriage. Amen.

(Drink the cup)

Jesus, fill us with Your Spirit. Unite us in Your love. Draw us deeper into the mystery of union with You—that we may be one as You and the Father are one. Teach us to love one another with Your supernatural love. Teach us to walk in Your ways. Teach us to see our marriage not only as partnership, but as a holy vessel that carries Your glory into this world.

We receive now—with faith and joy—the blessings You have promised. Blessings of peace, healing, provision, restoration, protection, wisdom, and overflowing grace. We stand in agreement, as one, declaring that no weapon formed against us shall prosper. We break every assignment of the enemy against our lives and marriage. We release blessings over our future, over our family, and over the generations to come.

Thank You, Jesus, for Your body and blood, given freely for us. We honor You, we love You, and we give You all the glory. In Your holy name we pray. Amen.

FINAL WORD

This week, practice holy listening. Slow your speech. Soften your tone. Notice what your spouse is really saying beneath the words. Remember, every conversation is an opportunity to love—and love, spoken with grace, can change everything.

WEEK 6
THE GIFT OF TOUCH—PHYSICAL AFFECTION AS SPIRITUAL CONNECTION

MEDITATION SCRIPTURES

"Therefore a man shall leave his father and mother and be joined to his wife, and they shall become one flesh."— Genesis 2:24 (NKJV)

"The husband should fulfill his marital duty to his wife, and likewise the wife to her husband. The wife does not have authority over her own body, but the husband does; likewise the husband does not have authority over his own body, but the wife does."— 1 Corinthians 7:3–4 (NASB)

"There's more to sex than mere skin on skin. Sex is as much spiritual mystery as physical fact. As written in Scripture, 'The two become one.'"—1 Corinthians 6:16 (MSG)

GUIDED MEDITATION ON SCRIPTURE

Sit quietly together, perhaps holding hands or placing a hand over each other's.

Read the scriptures aloud, slowly. Pause after each. Reflect silently:

- ﺱ How do we experience physical connection—not just sexually, but through touch, closeness, and presence?
- ﺱ Where have we grown cold or distant in affection?
- ﺱ Where is God inviting us to reclaim tenderness, attention, and physical presence?

Stay in quiet together for a few moments, simply resting in each other's nearness, inviting God into your physical bond.

QUOTE FOR TODAY

"The soul that is touched by love touches God, and in touching God touches all that is."

—*Meister Eckhart*

WORD FOR THE WEEK

God created us as embodied souls—spirit, mind, and body woven together. In marriage, physical affection is not just about sexual fulfillment; it is about presence, connection, and the language of love that transcends words. Holding hands, an embrace, a gentle touch on the shoulder—these small acts carry profound spiritual weight.

For many couples, life's pressures crowd out physical connection. Stress, fatigue, sickness, aging, resentment, or busyness can turn affection into an afterthought. But when we withdraw physically, even unintentionally, we create space for loneliness. And when we intentionally choose touch—not only sexually, but in daily, tender ways—we affirm, *"You are seen. You are loved. I am here."*

Sexual intimacy, too, is not just a physical act. It is a mystical participation in "one flesh," a joining of two souls that mirrors the union between Christ and the Church. When approached with reverence, tenderness, and joy, it becomes not merely an act of passion, but an act of worship—a holy and healing exchange of love.

This week, ask God to renew your physical connection. Pay attention to the small moments: the lingering hug, the gentle squeeze of a hand, the shared laughter. Remember, your bodies are not separate from your spiritual lives—they are part of the sacrament of marriage, the visible sign of an invisible grace.

PSALM TO MEDITATE ON

"You have hedged me behind and before, and laid Your hand upon me."—Psalm 139:5 (NKJV)

GUIDED MEDITATION ON THE PSALM

Read Psalm 139 aloud slowly.

Picture God's hand resting gently on your life, surrounding you with love.

Ask together:

- How can we offer God's kind of touch to one another this week?
- Where do we need to be gentler, more attentive, more present?

Breathe quietly for a moment, imagining God's loving touch flowing through your hands, renewing affection between you.

DECLARATIONS FOR THE WEEK

We declare:

- Our bodies are gifts to one another, holy and beloved.
- Our physical affection reflects the love of God.
- We honor one another with touch, tenderness, and joy.
- Our sexual intimacy is blessed and sanctified by God.
- We are one flesh, joined in covenant love.

COMMUNION PRAYER

(Prepare bread (or a cracker) and a small cup of juice. Together, hold the bread and pray).

Lord Jesus Christ, we come before You now, humbled and grateful. You are the Bread of Life, the true Manna from heaven. You gave Your body to be broken for us, that we might be made whole—spirit, soul, and body. You poured out Your blood as the cup of the new covenant, that we might be cleansed, forgiven, and reconciled to God.

We pause to remember Your sacrifice. We remember Your wounds, Your love, Your victory. We remember that You carried our sickness, our grief, our sins, and our shame upon Yourself at the cross (see Isaiah 53:4–5). You conquered death, hell, and the grave, and You rose again, so that we might share in Your life.

We confess, Lord, that we need You. We bring before You every place in our lives and marriage where we are weak, divided, hurting, or burdened. We ask for Your forgiveness for where we have spoken in anger, withheld love, carried resentment, or failed to honor one another. Wash us clean, Jesus—in Your mercy, cover us with Your righteousness.

As we eat this bread, we receive Your healing. Heal our hearts where they are wounded. Heal our minds where they are anxious or tormented. Heal our bodies where they are sick or weak. Heal our marriage where it has been strained or broken. Let the same power that raised You from the dead now flow through us. Jesus, thank You that You are the Living Word, full of grace and truth. As we eat this bread, we receive Your healing—over past wounds, over shame, over anything that has divided us physically or emotionally. As we drink this cup, we renew our covenant: to love, to serve, to cherish, to honor—in spirit, soul, and body.

(Eat the bread)

As we drink this cup, we renew our covenant with You and with each other. We declare that we are Yours, and You are ours. We belong to You—as individuals and as a couple. Strengthen the bond between us. Let our love be patient, kind, humble, and enduring. Let forgiveness flow freely in our home. Let Your peace reign over our household. Jesus, thank You for Your blood, poured out for forgiveness and new life. As we drink this cup, we receive Your forgiveness and the power to forgive each other. Bless our physical union. Renew our affection, our tenderness, our joy in one another. Let our love become a living sign of Your love for the world. Thank You, Jesus. Amen.

(Drink the cup)

Jesus, fill us with Your Spirit. Unite us in Your love. Draw us deeper into the mystery of union with You—that we may be one as You and the Father are one. Teach us to love one another with Your supernatural love. Teach us to walk in Your ways. Teach us to see our marriage not only as partnership, but as a holy vessel that carries Your glory into this world.

We receive now—with faith and joy—the blessings You have promised. Blessings of peace, healing, provision, restoration, protection, wisdom, and overflowing grace. We stand in agreement, as one, declaring that no weapon formed against us shall prosper. We break every assignment of the enemy against our lives and marriage. We release blessings over our future, over our family, and over the generations to come.

Jesus, thank You for taking on flesh, for becoming Emmanuel—God with us. Thank You that You sanctify not only our souls but also our bodies, making them temples of Your Spirit.

Thank You, Jesus, for Your body and blood, given freely for us. We honor You, we love You, and we give You all the glory. In Your holy name we pray. Amen.

FINAL WORD

This week, let affection be your prayer. Small touches, quiet presence, shared laughter—these are the ways love is woven back together, thread by holy thread. Let God's love flow through your hands, and watch what He heals.

WEEK 7
WHEN DREAMS ARE DELAYED—
HOLDING HOPE TOGETHER

MEDITATION SCRIPTURES

"Hope deferred makes the heart sick, but when the desire comes, it is a tree of life."—Proverbs 13:12 (NKJV)

"Let us hold tightly without wavering to the hope we affirm, for God can be trusted to keep His promise."—Hebrews 10:23 (NLT)

"But if we hope for what we do not see, we eagerly wait for it with perseverance."—Romans 8:25 (NASB)

GUIDED MEDITATION ON SCRIPTURE

Sit together quietly. Take a few slow breaths.

Read the scriptures aloud, slowly. Let the words settle in your heart: **hope deferred… hold tightly to hope… wait with perseverance.**

Ask silently:

- ﺱ What dream or desire have we been waiting for?
- ﺱ Where have we felt disappointment, weariness, or doubt?

ی How is God inviting us to hold hope—not alone, but together?

Rest in the quiet, letting God gently lift the weight of waiting from your shoulders.

QUOTE FOR TODAY

"We shall steer safely through every storm, so long as our heart is right, our intention fervent, our courage steadfast, and our trust fixed on God."

—*St. Francis de Sales*

WORD FOR THE WEEK

Every marriage holds dreams—some spoken, some hidden. Dreams for children, for healing, for a home, for ministry, for reconciliation, for breakthrough. But what happens when those dreams are delayed? When months turn to years, and prayers seem to echo into silence?

Scripture acknowledges the pain of deferred hope. It makes the heart sick, weary, and tempted to shut down. Couples may start avoiding the subject, carrying private grief, or even blaming one another. But God does not call us to carry deferred dreams in isolation. He invites us to hold hope—not with forced optimism, but with shared trust in His faithfulness.

Waiting together becomes a sacred act. It is an agreement to believe that God is still good, even when the story is not unfolding as we imagined. It is a choice to comfort one another instead of criticize, to pray together instead of pulling apart, to bless the present even as we long for the future.

This week, name the places where you are still waiting. Lay them openly before God, as an offering. Ask for fresh courage to hold hope, together—not clinging to outcomes, but clinging to the One who holds your future.

PSALM TO MEDITATE ON

"I would have lost heart, unless I had believed that I would see the goodness of the Lord in the land of the living. Wait on the Lord; be of good courage, and He shall strengthen your heart; wait, I say, on the Lord!"—Psalm 27:13–14 (NKJV)

GUIDED MEDITATION ON THE PSALM

Read Psalm 27 aloud slowly.

Picture yourselves waiting—not in despair, but in quiet trust.

Ask together:

- ᔑ Lord, where do we need courage to keep waiting?
- ᔑ How can we bless and strengthen each other in the waiting?

Sit for a moment in stillness, receiving His strengthening presence.

DECLARATIONS FOR THE WEEK

We declare:

- God is faithful, even in the waiting.
- Our hearts will not lose hope, for we trust in His goodness.
- We wait together, not alone—strengthened by love.
- We bless the present moment, even as we hope for the future.
- We will see the goodness of the Lord in the land of the living.

COMMUNION PRAYER

(Prepare bread (or a cracker) and a small cup of juice. Together, hold the bread and pray).

Lord Jesus Christ, we come before You now, humbled and grateful. You are the Bread of Life, the true Manna from heaven. You gave Your body to be broken for us, that we might be made whole—spirit, soul, and body. You poured out Your blood as the cup of the new covenant, that we might be cleansed, forgiven, and reconciled to God.

We pause to remember Your sacrifice. We remember Your wounds, Your love, Your victory. We remember that You carried our sickness, our grief, our sins, and our shame upon Yourself at the cross (see Isaiah 53:4–5). You conquered death, hell, and the grave, and You rose again, so that we might share in Your life.

We confess, Lord, that we need You. We bring before You every place in our lives and marriage where we are weak, divided, hurting, or burdened. We ask for Your forgiveness for where we have spoken in anger, withheld love, carried resentment, or failed to honor one another. Wash us clean, Jesus—in Your mercy, cover us with Your righteousness.

As we eat this bread, we receive Your healing. Heal our hearts where they are wounded. Heal our minds where they are anxious or tormented. Heal our bodies where they are sick or weak. Heal our marriage where it has been strained or broken. Let the same power that raised You from the dead now flow through us. Jesus, You know what it is to wait. You waited for the cross. You waited for resurrection. You wait now for the full redemption of all things. As we eat this bread, we surrender our waiting to You.

(Eat the bread)

As we drink this cup, we renew our covenant with You and with each other. We declare that we are Yours, and You are ours. We belong to You—as individuals and as a couple. Strengthen the bond between us. Let our love be patient, kind, humble, and enduring. Let forgiveness flow freely in our home. Let Your peace reign over our household. Jesus, thank You for Your blood, poured out for forgiveness and new life. As we drink this cup, we trust Your timing, Your goodness, Your plan. We lay down every deferred hope, every unfulfilled dream, every unanswered prayer. We receive instead Your presence—here, now—as our deepest joy.

(Drink the cup)

Jesus, fill us with Your Spirit. Unite us in Your love. Draw us deeper into the mystery of union with You—that we may be one as You and the Father are one. Teach us to love one another with Your supernatural love. Teach us to walk in Your ways. Teach us to see our marriage not only as partnership, but as a holy vessel that carries Your glory into this world.

We receive now—with faith and joy—the blessings You have promised. Blessings of peace, healing, provision, restoration, protection, wisdom, and overflowing grace. We stand in agreement, as one, declaring that no weapon formed against us shall prosper. We break every assignment of the enemy against our lives and marriage. We release blessings over our future, over our family, and over the generations to come.

Strengthen us, Lord. Teach us to wait with courage, and to love each other well in the waiting.

Thank You, Jesus, for Your body and blood, given freely for us. We honor You, we love You, and we give You all the glory. In Your holy name we pray. Amen.

FINAL WORD

Waiting does not mean absence; it means trust. You are not waiting alone. God is with you, pouring His goodness into every unseen place. Hold hope—not perfectly, but together—and you will find Him faithful.

WEEK 8
SACRIFICIAL LOVE—LAYING DOWN MY LIFE FOR YOU

MEDITATION SCRIPTURES

"Greater love has no one than this, than to lay down one's life for his friends."—John 15:13 (NKJV)

"Husbands, love your wives, just as Christ also loved the church and gave Himself for her."—Ephesians 5:25 (NKJV)

"If you've gotten anything at all out of following Christ, if His love has made any difference in your life... Don't push your way to the front; don't sweet-talk your way to the top. Put yourself aside, and help others get ahead."—Philippians 2:1, 3–4 (MSG)

GUIDED MEDITATION ON SCRIPTURE

Sit quietly together. Take a few slow breaths.

Read the scriptures aloud, slowly, pausing after each. Reflect silently:

- ﺱ What does "laying down my life" look like in our daily marriage?
- ﺱ Where am I being invited to love more selflessly?

- How has my spouse loved me in ways I may not have noticed or acknowledged?

Stay in the quiet, thanking God for moments of sacrificial love you've already shared—and inviting Him to teach you more.

QUOTE FOR TODAY

"Love that does not know of suffering is not worthy of the name."

—Meister Eckhart

WORD FOR THE WEEK

We often think of sacrificial love as heroic, dramatic, or a once-in-a-lifetime experience. But in marriage, sacrificial love is made of small, daily choices: letting go of pride, forgiving first, holding your tongue, offering help without being asked, putting your spouse's needs above your own, and showing up when you're tired.

This love does not erase self; it fulfills it. In laying down selfishness, we make room for deeper joy, connection, and purpose. Jesus' love for us is the model: not sentimental, but costly; not self-centered, but self-giving; not occasional, but constant.

Marriage invites both husband and wife into this divine pattern. Ephesians 5 calls husbands to love their wives as Christ loved the church, but wives, too, are invited to practice Christ-like love, laying down fear, control, or resentment, and choosing trust, respect, and service.

This week, ask God to open your eyes to opportunities for small acts of sacrifice and also to help you recognize and honor the ways your spouse is already laying down their life in love. These holy exchanges are not wasted; they are the hidden glory of marriage.

PSALM TO MEDITATE ON

"Offer the sacrifices of righteousness, and put your trust in the Lord."—Psalm 4:5 (NKJV)

GUIDED MEDITATION ON THE PSALM

Read Psalm 4:5 aloud slowly.

Ask together:

- Lord, where are You calling us to offer sacrifices of love and righteousness this week?
- How can we trust You more deeply as we lay ourselves down for each other?

Sit quietly, imagining these sacrifices not as burdens, but as gifts you are offering freely, out of love.

DECLARATIONS FOR THE WEEK

We declare:

- We are learning to love with Christ-like sacrifice.
- Our marriage is marked by humility, service, and trust.
- We lay down selfishness and receive God's joy.

ﲾ We honor and cherish the daily sacrifices we make for one another.

ﲾ Our love reflects the love of Jesus to the world.

COMMUNION PRAYER

(Prepare bread (or a cracker) and a small cup of juice. Together, hold the bread and pray).

Lord Jesus Christ, we come before You now, humbled and grateful. You are the Bread of Life, the true Manna from heaven. You gave Your body to be broken for us, that we might be made whole—spirit, soul, and body. You poured out Your blood as the cup of the new covenant, that we might be cleansed, forgiven, and reconciled to God.

We pause to remember Your sacrifice. We remember Your wounds, Your love, Your victory. We remember that You carried our sickness, our grief, our sins, and our shame upon Yourself at the cross (see Isaiah 53:4–5). You conquered death, hell, and the grave, and You rose again, so that we might share in Your life.

We confess, Lord, that we need You. We bring before You every place in our lives and marriage where we are weak, divided, hurting, or burdened. We ask for Your forgiveness for where we have spoken in anger, withheld love, carried resentment, or failed to honor one another. Wash us clean, Jesus—in Your mercy, cover us with Your righteousness.

As we eat this bread, we receive Your healing. Heal our hearts where they are wounded. Heal our minds where they are anxious or

tormented. Heal our bodies where they are sick or weak. Heal our marriage where it has been strained or broken. Let the same power that raised You from the dead now flow through us. Jesus, You laid down Your life, not out of duty, but out of love. You gave Your body to heal us. You poured out Your blood to reconcile us to God. As we eat this bread, we receive Your love—the love that transforms, heals, and empowers us.

(Eat the bread)

As we drink this cup, we renew our covenant with You and with each other. We declare that we are Yours, and You are ours. We belong to You—as individuals and as a couple. Strengthen the bond between us. Let our love be patient, kind, humble, and enduring. Let forgiveness flow freely in our home. Let Your peace reign over our household. Jesus, thank You for Your blood, poured out for forgiveness and new life. As we drink this cup, we renew our covenant—with You and with each other—to love as You love.

(Drink the cup)

Jesus, fill us with Your Spirit. Unite us in Your love. Draw us deeper into the mystery of union with You—that we may be one as You and the Father are one. Teach us to love one another with Your supernatural love. Teach us to walk in Your ways. Teach us to see our marriage not only as partnership, but as a holy vessel that carries Your glory into this world.

We receive now—with faith and joy—the blessings You have promised. Blessings of peace, healing, provision, restoration, protection, wisdom, and overflowing grace. We stand in agreement, as one, declaring that no weapon formed against us shall prosper. We break every assignment of the enemy against our lives and marriage. We release blessings over our future, over our family, and over the generations to come.

Help us, Lord, to lay down selfishness, to choose kindness, to serve with joy, and to forgive with grace. Let our marriage be a picture of Your sacrificial love, shining light in a world that is desperate to see it.

Thank You, Jesus. Amen.

FINAL WORD

Sacrificial love is not about losing yourself; it's about finding the deeper self God created—the one capable of great love, great courage, and great joy. This week, lean into that love. It will change everything.

WEEK 9
PRAYER AS A COUPLE—TWO VOICES, ONE HEART

MEDITATION SCRIPTURES

"Again I say to you that if two of you agree on earth concerning anything that they ask, it will be done for them by My Father in heaven. For where two or three are gathered together in My name, I am there in the midst of them."—Matthew 18:19–20 (NKJV)

"Devote yourselves to prayer, keeping alert in it with an attitude of thanksgiving."—Colossians 4:2 (NASB)

"If we confess our sins, He is faithful and just to forgive us and to cleanse us from all unrighteousness."—1 John 1:9 (NKJV)

GUIDED MEDITATION ON SCRIPTURE

Sit quietly together. Take a few slow, deep breaths.

Read the scriptures aloud, letting the words settle over you: agreeing together, gathering in His name, devotion to prayer, confession, and cleansing.

Reflect silently:

- ﺱ How often do we pray together, not just over meals or needs, but heart to heart?
- ﺱ What has held us back from praying together more deeply?
- ﺱ How might our marriage change if prayer became a shared rhythm, not a rare event?

Sit in quiet openness, inviting God into this part of your relationship.

QUOTE FOR TODAY

"Prayer is nothing else than being on terms of friendship with God."
—*Teresa of Ávila*

WORD FOR THE WEEK

Prayer is one of the simplest and most intimate practices couples can share—and often, one of the most neglected. For many, praying together feels awkward, vulnerable, or unfamiliar. But prayer was never meant to be a performance; it is the honest offering of our hearts to God, together.

When we pray as a couple, we open space not only for God to work, but for us to understand one another more deeply. We hear each other's worries, longings, hopes, and gratitude. We stand shoulder to shoulder before the One who knows us fully and loves us completely. In those moments, something shifts—not just between us and God, but between us as spouses.

Prayer does not have to be long or eloquent. It can be as simple as holding hands and saying, *"God, help us,"* or *"Thank You for today,"* or *"We need You in this."* Over time, prayer becomes a rhythm—a safe place where love grows deeper and trust grows stronger.

This week, step into the practice of praying together. It may feel small at first, but its power is great. Invite Jesus into your conversations, struggles, hopes, and ordinary days. You will find that He is already there, waiting.

PSALM TO MEDITATE ON

"Hear my cry, O God; attend to my prayer. From the end of the earth I will cry to You, when my heart is overwhelmed; lead me to the rock that is higher than I."—Psalm 61:1–2 (NKJV)

GUIDED MEDITATION ON THE PSALM

Read Psalm 61:1-2 aloud slowly.

Ask together:

- Where do we need God's help right now?
- Where have we been trying to carry things alone?

Imagine Jesus as the "rock higher than we are"—steady, safe, strong. Picture yourselves standing together on that Rock, lifted above fear or overwhelm.

DECLARATIONS FOR THE WEEK

We declare:

- ☙ Our marriage is grounded in prayer and trust in God.
- ☙ We are learning to pray with honesty, humility, and love.
- ☙ God hears us when we pray—together or apart.
- ☙ Prayer strengthens our bond and invites God's peace into our home.
- ☙ We will not carry burdens alone; we will bring them to the Lord, together.

COMMUNION PRAYER

(Prepare bread (or a cracker) and a small cup of juice. Together, hold the bread and pray).

Lord Jesus Christ, we come before You now, humbled and grateful. You are the Bread of Life, the true Manna from heaven. You gave Your body to be broken for us, that we might be made whole—spirit, soul, and body. You poured out Your blood as the cup of the new covenant, that we might be cleansed, forgiven, and reconciled to God.

We pause to remember Your sacrifice. We remember Your wounds, Your love, Your victory. We remember that You carried our sickness, our grief, our sins, and our shame upon Yourself at the cross (see Isaiah 53:4–5). You conquered death, hell, and the grave, and You rose again, so that we might share in Your life.

We confess, Lord, that we need You. We bring before You every place in our lives and marriage where we are weak, divided, hurting, or burdened. We ask for Your forgiveness for where we have spoken in anger, withheld love, carried resentment, or failed to honor one another. Wash us clean, Jesus—in Your mercy, cover us with Your righteousness.

As we eat this bread, we receive Your healing. Heal our hearts where they are wounded. Heal our minds where they are anxious or tormented. Heal our bodies where they are sick or weak. Heal our marriage where it has been strained or broken. Let the same power that raised You from the dead now flow through us. Jesus, thank You that when we come together in Your name, You are here among us. As we eat this bread, we remember Your body given for us—not only for our salvation, but for our healing, our unity, and our peace.

(Eat the bread)

As we drink this cup, we renew our covenant with You and with each other. We declare that we are Yours, and You are ours. We belong to You—as individuals and as a couple. Strengthen the bond between us. Let our love be patient, kind, humble, and enduring. Let forgiveness flow freely in our home. Let Your peace reign over our household. Jesus, thank You for Your blood, poured out for forgiveness and new life. As we drink this cup, we receive the cleansing of Your blood—washing over every area where we've fallen short, renewing us, and binding us together in Your love.

(Drink the cup)

Jesus, fill us with Your Spirit. Unite us in Your love. Draw us deeper into the mystery of union with You—that we may be one as You and the Father are one. Teach us to love one another with Your supernatural love. Teach us to walk in Your ways. Teach us to see our marriage not only as partnership, but as a holy vessel that carries Your glory into this world.

We receive now—with faith and joy—the blessings You have promised. Blessings of peace, healing, provision, restoration, protection, wisdom, and overflowing grace. We stand in agreement, as one, declaring that no weapon formed against us shall prosper. We break every assignment of the enemy against our lives and marriage. We release blessings over our future, over our family, and over the generations to come.

Teach us to pray, Lord—not with fancy words, but with open hearts. Make our marriage a house of prayer, a place where heaven meets earth, where love is strengthened, and where Your presence abides.

Thank You, Jesus. Amen.

FINAL WORD

You do not need to pray perfectly—only honestly. Start small. Hold hands. Speak a few simple words. Listen. Let prayer become part of the air you breathe as a couple, and watch how God meets you there.

WEEK 10
OVERCOMING FEAR—FAITH IN THE FACE OF UNCERTAINTY

MEDITATION SCRIPTURES

"For God has not given us a spirit of fear, but of power and of love and of a sound mind." —2 Timothy 1:7 (NKJV)

"Even though I walk through the valley of the shadow of death, I will fear no evil, for You are with me; Your rod and Your staff, they comfort me."—Psalm 23:4 (NASB)

"So we can say with confidence, 'The Lord is my helper, so I will have no fear. What can mere people do to me?'"—Hebrews 13:6 (NLT)

GUIDED MEDITATION ON SCRIPTURE

Sit quietly together, holding hands or resting in stillness side by side.

Read the scriptures aloud, slowly. After each verse, pause and let the words settle in: **no spirit of fear... I will fear no evil... the Lord is my helper.**

Reflect silently:

- ك What are we afraid of right now—together or individually?
- ك How have we been trying to control what we fear instead of surrendering it?
- ك What would it feel like to place that fear into God's hands?

Breathe quietly and imagine God's peace settling over you both.

QUOTE FOR TODAY

"All shall be well, and all shall be well, and all manner of thing shall be well."

—*Julian of Norwich*

WORD FOR THE WEEK

Fear comes with every marriage. Fear of loss, of sickness, of financial lack, of betrayal, of the unknown future. It whispers in the middle of the night and creeps in when life feels unstable. And left unchecked, fear divides—it isolates, hardens, and steals peace.

But Scripture reminds us that fear is not from God. He gives us a spirit of power, love, and a sound mind. He walks with us through the darkest valleys. He surrounds us with His presence, so we do not have to face uncertainty alone.

In marriage, overcoming fear is not about pretending it doesn't exist—it's about facing it together, hand in hand, and lifting it up to

God. It's about confessing our worries out loud, praying over them, and choosing to stand in faith, even when the outcome is unclear.

This week, bring your fears into the light—not to shame them, but to surrender them. Speak them, pray over them, and then, together, declare: **"The Lord is our helper. We will not fear."** In that surrender, you will find new strength, deeper unity, and God's peace breaking through.

PSALM TO MEDITATE ON

"I sought the Lord, and He heard me, and delivered me from all my fears."—Psalm 34:4 (NKJV)

GUIDED MEDITATION ON THE PSALM

Read Psalm 34 aloud slowly.

Ask together:

- ﺹ Lord, what fear are You inviting us to release this week?
- ﺹ What promise are You giving us in exchange?

Sit quietly, picturing God lifting those fears from your hands and filling you with courage.

DECLARATIONS FOR THE WEEK

We declare:

- ی God has not given us a spirit of fear, but of power, love, and a sound mind.
- ی We will not walk in fear, for the Lord is with us.
- ی Our marriage is guarded by God's presence and peace.
- ی We surrender every worry to Him and stand together in faith.
- ی We are strong, united, and courageous in Christ.

COMMUNION PRAYER

(Prepare bread (or a cracker) and a small cup of juice. Together, hold the bread and pray).

Lord Jesus Christ, we come before You now, humbled and grateful. You are the Bread of Life, the true Manna from heaven. You gave Your body to be broken for us, that we might be made whole—spirit, soul, and body. You poured out Your blood as the cup of the new covenant, that we might be cleansed, forgiven, and reconciled to God.

We pause to remember Your sacrifice. We remember Your wounds, Your love, Your victory. We remember that You carried our sickness, our grief, our sins, and our shame upon Yourself at the cross (see Isaiah 53:4–5). You conquered death, hell, and the grave, and You rose again, so that we might share in Your life.

We confess, Lord, that we need You. We bring before You every place in our lives and marriage where we are weak, divided, hurting, or burdened. We ask for Your forgiveness for where we have spoken in anger, withheld love, carried resentment, or failed to honor one another. Wash us clean, Jesus—in Your mercy, cover us with Your righteousness.

As we eat this bread, we receive Your healing. Heal our hearts where they are wounded. Heal our minds where they are anxious or tormented. Heal our bodies where they are sick or weak. Heal our marriage where it has been strained or broken. Let the same power that raised You from the dead now flow through us. As we eat this bread, we receive Your strength in place of our weakness.

(Eat the bread)

As we drink this cup, we renew our covenant with You and with each other. We declare that we are Yours, and You are ours. We belong to You—as individuals and as a couple. Strengthen the bond between us. Let our love be patient, kind, humble, and enduring. Let forgiveness flow freely in our home. Let Your peace reign over our household. Jesus, thank You for Your blood, poured out for forgiveness and new life. As we drink this cup, we receive Your peace where there has been fear.

(Drink the cup)

Jesus, fill us with Your Spirit. Unite us in Your love. Draw us deeper into the mystery of union with You—that we may be one as You and

the Father are one. Teach us to love one another with Your supernatural love. Teach us to walk in Your ways. Teach us to see our marriage not only as partnership, but as a holy vessel that carries Your glory into this world.

We receive now—with faith and joy—the blessings You have promised. Blessings of peace, healing, provision, restoration, protection, wisdom, and overflowing grace. We stand in agreement, as one, declaring that no weapon formed against us shall prosper. We break every assignment of the enemy against our lives and marriage. We release blessings over our future, over our family, and over the generations to come.

We lay down our anxieties at Your feet. We take up the armor of faith. We declare over our marriage and our home: Jesus is Lord. His peace rules here. We are not afraid.

Thank You, Jesus. Amen.

FINAL WORD

Fear shrinks when it is named, prayed over, and surrendered. This week, be brave enough to speak your fears to each other, and even braver to hand them over to God. His love will carry you through.

COUPLES EXERCISE AND ACTIVITY

NAMING, SURRENDERING, AND REPLACING FEAR

NAMING THE FEAR (HEART SHARING)

Set aside 20–30 minutes when you can be alone, undistracted, and unhurried. Sit face to face, holding hands or sitting close, and take a deep breath together.

One at a time, share:

- "What am I afraid of right now?" (Examples: losing a job, health issues, drifting apart, finances, children, aging, disappointment, etc.)

- "How is this fear affecting me or us?" (Examples: making me anxious, making me withdraw, making me control things, making me irritable, etc.)

Important: Just listen. No fixing. No correcting. No minimizing. Just hear and hold.

SURRENDERING THE FEAR (PRAY TOGETHER)

When both have shared, pray together:

- Start with thanks. *"Jesus, thank You that You are here with us right now."*

- Surrender the fears. *"We give You these fears we have shared. We can't carry them or control them. We place them into Your hands."*

- Ask for exchange. *"Fill us with Your peace, Your wisdom, Your courage, and Your love."*

- Speak blessing over each other. Lay a hand gently on each other's shoulder or head and say, *"I bless you to walk in God's peace. You are not alone. I am with you. God is with you."*

REPLACING THE FEAR (FAITH ANCHOR ACTIVITY)

Together, write one statement of faith to carry into the week.

For example:

- *"God is our provider; we will not fear lack."*
- *"The Lord is our helper; we will not fear the future."*
- *"We are united; we will not fear division."*
- *"Jesus is our healer; we will not fear sickness."*

Write it on a note, sticky, or card and place it somewhere you will both see it daily, such as on the bathroom mirror, fridge, bedside table, or even as your phone wallpaper.

Every time fear rises this week, speak this faith anchor statement out loud together.

If you want, you can also choose a small physical symbol (like a smooth stone, a cross, a candle, or a written word) to remind you of God's presence and peace.

Keep it somewhere visible as a reminder that fear has been surrendered, and faith is holding you steady.

WHY THIS ACTIVITY MATTERS

- ی It builds emotional intimacy by making space for honest, non-judgmental sharing.
- ی It invites God directly into your struggles, replacing anxiety with trust.
- ی It gives you something tangible (words and symbols) to hold onto during the week.
- ی It reframes fear as a place of connection, not division between you.

TRIALS AND STRUGGLES

(sickness, barrenness, grief, fatigue, finances)

WEEK 11
BARRENNESS AND FRUITFULNESS— TRUSTING GOD WITH THE UNSEEN

MEDITATION SCRIPTURES

"He gives the childless woman a family, making her a happy mother. Praise the Lord!"—Psalm 113:9 (NLT)

"Sing, O barren, you who have not borne! Break forth into singing, and cry aloud... For more are the children of the desolate than the children of the married woman."—Isaiah 54:1 (NKJV)

"Blessed is the man who trusts in the Lord, and whose hope is the Lord. For he shall be like a tree planted by the waters... and will not be anxious in the year of drought, nor will cease from yielding fruit."—Jeremiah 17:7–8 (NKJV)

GUIDED MEDITATION ON SCRIPTURE

Sit quietly together, holding hands or sitting side by side.

Read the scriptures aloud slowly, allowing space for silence between each one.

Let the words *trust, hope, sing, fruitfulness* settle in your hearts.

Reflect silently:

- ﺱ What areas of our life feel barren, empty, or delayed?
- ﺱ Where are we longing to see God's promise fulfilled—in children, dreams, healing, purpose, ministry, or other desires?
- ﺱ Where is God inviting us to trust Him with what we cannot yet see?

Breathe in His peace; breathe out your fears.

QUOTE FOR TODAY

"What God removes He replaces with Himself."

—*Julian of Norwich*

WORD FOR THE WEEK

Barrenness is not only about the absence of children—it is any area where we long for fruitfulness but face emptiness. For some couples, it is the pain of infertility. For others, it is the ache of unanswered prayers, stalled dreams, or promises that seem delayed beyond hope.

The Bible does not shy away from stories of barrenness—Sarah, Rebekah, Hannah, Elizabeth. Nor does it dismiss their longing. Yet in every story, God works not only in the outcome, but in the waiting. Sometimes He brings a miracle. Sometimes He brings Himself. And sometimes, mysteriously, He brings both.

Trusting God in barren places is not passive. It is an active surrender: worshipping when you feel empty, holding hands when you feel isolated, and choosing to believe that fruitfulness comes in many forms—seen and unseen. Sometimes the unseen fruit is the deepest: trust, resilience, love, intimacy, faith.

This week, bring your barren places before God, not to demand a timetable, but to open your hearts afresh. Let Him show you where He is already planting seeds of life. Remember, with Him, no place is truly barren.

PSALM TO MEDITATE ON

"Those who sow in tears shall reap in joy. He who continually goes forth weeping, bearing seed for sowing, shall doubtless come again with rejoicing, bringing his sheaves with him."—Psalm 126:5–6 (NKJV)

GUIDED MEDITATION ON THE PSALM

Read Psalm 126 slowly.

Ask together:

- ﺱ What have we been sowing in tears?
- ﺱ What joy, hope, or fruit might God be preparing in hidden places?

Sit in stillness, imagining God tenderly gathering your tears, planting them as seeds.

DECLARATIONS FOR THE WEEK

We declare:

- ﯼ God is with us in barren places and in fruitful places.
- ﯼ We trust His timing, His goodness, and His love.
- ﯼ Our marriage is bearing unseen fruit even now.
- ﯼ We are hopeful, resilient, and surrendered.
- ﯼ We will rejoice, knowing that no seed is wasted in God's hands.

COMMUNION PRAYER

(Prepare bread (or a cracker) and a small cup of juice. Together, hold the bread and pray).

Lord Jesus Christ, we come before You now, humbled and grateful. You are the Bread of Life, the true Manna from heaven. You gave Your body to be broken for us, that we might be made whole—spirit, soul, and body. You poured out Your blood as the cup of the new covenant, that we might be cleansed, forgiven, and reconciled to God.

We pause to remember Your sacrifice. We remember Your wounds, Your love, Your victory. We remember that You carried our sickness, our grief, our sins, and our shame upon Yourself at the cross (see Isaiah 53:4–5). You conquered death, hell, and the grave, and You rose again, so that we might share in Your life.

We confess, Lord, that we need You. We bring before You every place in our lives and marriage where we are weak, divided, hurting, or

burdened. We ask for Your forgiveness for where we have spoken in anger, withheld love, carried resentment, or failed to honor one another. Wash us clean, Jesus—in Your mercy, cover us with Your righteousness.

As we eat this bread, we receive Your healing. Heal our hearts where they are wounded. Heal our minds where they are anxious or tormented. Heal our bodies where they are sick or weak. Heal our marriage where it has been strained or broken. Let the same power that raised You from the dead now flow through us. Jesus, You are the God who brings life from the dead, hope from despair, and fruitfulness from barren places. You are the Resurrection and the Life. As we eat this bread, we remember Your body—broken to make all things new.

(Eat the bread)

As we drink this cup, we renew our covenant with You and with each other. We declare that we are Yours, and You are ours. We belong to You—as individuals and as a couple. Strengthen the bond between us. Let our love be patient, kind, humble, and enduring. Let forgiveness flow freely in our home. Let Your peace reign over our household. Jesus, thank You for Your blood, poured out for forgiveness and new life. As we drink this cup, we receive Your blood—poured out to bring healing, restoration, and new beginnings.

(Drink the cup)

Jesus, fill us with Your Spirit. Unite us in Your love. Draw us deeper into the mystery of union with You—that we may be one as You and the Father are one. Teach us to love one another with Your supernatural love. Teach us to walk in Your ways. Teach us to see our marriage not only as partnership, but as a holy vessel that carries Your glory into this world.

We receive now—with faith and joy—the blessings You have promised. Blessings of peace, healing, provision, restoration, protection, wisdom, and overflowing grace. We stand in agreement, as one, declaring that no weapon formed against us shall prosper. We break every assignment of the enemy against our lives and marriage. We release blessings over our future, over our family, and over the generations to come.

We place every longing, every unfulfilled hope, every barren place into Your hands. We trust You, Jesus. We ask You to fill our home with Your life, Your love, and Your fruitfulness—whatever shape that takes.

Amen.

FINAL WORD

Barren seasons are never wasted in God's kingdom. In His hands, every tear becomes a seed, every waiting season becomes preparation, and every longing becomes a doorway to deeper love. Trust Him to bring life in His way, in His time.

WEEK 12
REDEEMING THE PAST—GOD'S GRACE OVER MISTAKES AND SINS

MEDITATION SCRIPTURES

"Therefore, if anyone is in Christ, he is a new creation; old things have passed away; behold, all things have become new."—2 Corinthians 5:17 (NKJV)

"Come now, and let us reason together, says the Lord, 'Though your sins are like scarlet, they shall be as white as snow; though they are red like crimson, they shall be as wool.'"—Isaiah 1:18 (NKJV)

"For I will be merciful toward their iniquities, and I will remember their sins no more."—Hebrews 8:12 (NASB)

GUIDED MEDITATION ON SCRIPTURE

Sit together quietly. Take a few deep, slow breaths.

Read the scriptures aloud, slowly. Let the words *new creation… white as snow… remember sins no more* soak into your hearts.

Reflect silently:

- ی What mistakes or regrets from the past still weigh on our hearts or marriage?
- ی What have we struggled to fully receive forgiveness for— from God, from each other, or from ourselves?
- ی What would it feel like to let grace have the final word over our past?

Rest in the quiet, inviting God to cover your past with His mercy.

QUOTE FOR TODAY

"The soul which has come to the knowledge of God by love does not dwell upon her past sins but on the mercy of Him who has forgiven her."

—*Catherine of Siena*

WORD FOR THE WEEK

Every marriage carries a past. There are chapters we cherish and chapters we wish we could erase. Some are personal, some are shared, some were buried long ago. But no matter how hidden or painful, nothing from the past is too great for God to redeem.

Scripture doesn't pretend sin has no cost, but it proclaims that grace has the final say. In Christ, we are made new, not by denying our failures, but by bringing them into His light and letting Him transform them. For couples, this means no longer defining each other by old mistakes, past betrayals, or old wounds. It means seeing one another as God sees us: forgiven, beloved, and in a process of growth.

It also means forgiving yourself. Many carry shame or regret from before marriage—past relationships, abortions, addictions, or failures they never confessed. But Jesus says, **"Though your sins are like scarlet, they shall be white as snow."** He remembers your sins no more. And as you let go of what He has let go of, you step into new freedom—personally and together.

This week, open the door to healing. Name the past, not to punish each other or yourself, but to release it into the hands of the only One who can redeem it. Grace is stronger than your history. It is the river that carries you both forward.

PSALM TO MEDITATE ON

"Bless the Lord, O my soul, and forget not all His benefits: Who forgives all your iniquities, Who heals all your diseases, Who redeems your life from destruction, Who crowns you with lovingkindness and tender mercies."—Psalm 103:2–4 (NKJV)

GUIDED MEDITATION ON THE PSALM

Read Psalm 103 aloud slowly.

Ask together:

> ৬ Lord, what are You forgiving, healing, or redeeming in us today?

ی Where do we need to let Your mercy rewrite our story?

Imagine God's lovingkindness covering you both like a crown, marking you as His.

DECLARATIONS FOR THE WEEK

We declare:

- ی We are not defined by our past; we are defined by God's grace.
- ی Our marriage is a place of forgiveness, healing, and new beginnings.
- ی We release each other from old wounds, old mistakes, and old identities.
- ی We forgive ourselves, knowing Christ has forgiven us.
- ی We walk forward in freedom, mercy, and hope.

COMMUNION PRAYER

(Prepare bread (or a cracker) and a small cup of juice. Together, hold the bread and pray).

Lord Jesus Christ, we come before You now, humbled and grateful. You are the Bread of Life, the true Manna from heaven. You gave Your body to be broken for us, that we might be made whole—spirit, soul, and body. You poured out Your blood as the cup of the new covenant, that we might be cleansed, forgiven, and reconciled to God.

We pause to remember Your sacrifice. We remember Your wounds, Your love, Your victory. We remember that You carried our sickness, our grief, our sins, and our shame upon Yourself at the cross (see Isaiah 53:4–5). You conquered death, hell, and the grave, and You rose again, so that we might share in Your life.

We confess, Lord, that we need You. We bring before You every place in our lives and marriage where we are weak, divided, hurting, or burdened. We ask for Your forgiveness for where we have spoken in anger, withheld love, carried resentment, or failed to honor one another. Wash us clean, Jesus—in Your mercy, cover us with Your righteousness.

As we eat this bread, we receive Your healing. Heal our hearts where they are wounded. Heal our minds where they are anxious or tormented. Heal our bodies where they are sick or weak. Heal our marriage where it has been strained or broken. Let the same power that raised You from the dead now flow through us. Jesus, thank You for Your body, broken to heal our brokenness. Thank You for Your blood, poured out to forgive every sin—past, present, and future. As we eat this bread, we receive Your healing over every place the past has left a mark.

(Eat the bread)

As we drink this cup, we renew our covenant with You and with each other. We declare that we are Yours, and You are ours. We belong to You—as individuals and as a couple. Strengthen the bond between us. Let our love be patient, kind, humble, and enduring. Let forgiveness flow freely in our home. Let Your peace reign over our household. Jesus, thank You for Your blood, poured out for forgiveness and new life. As we drink this cup, we receive Your cleansing, Your redemption, Your freedom.

(Drink the cup)

Jesus, fill us with Your Spirit. Unite us in Your love. Draw us deeper into the mystery of union with You—that we may be one as You and the Father are one. Teach us to love one another with Your supernatural love. Teach us to walk in Your ways. Teach us to see our marriage not only as partnership, but as a holy vessel that carries Your glory into this world.

We receive now—with faith and joy—the blessings You have promised. Blessings of peace, healing, provision, restoration, protection, wisdom, and overflowing grace. We stand in agreement, as one, declaring that no weapon formed against us shall prosper. We break every assignment of the enemy against our lives and marriage. We release blessings over our future, over our family, and over the generations to come.

We release old wounds, regrets, and accusations into Your hands. We declare over our marriage: we are a new creation in You. We are covered by mercy. We are crowned with love.

Thank You, Jesus. Amen.

FINAL WORD

Grace does not erase the past; it transforms it. Let God take your broken pieces, and you will find that nothing—no failure, no regret—is wasted in His hands.

COUPLES ACTIVITY: "THE LET-GO PRAYER"

Write (or speak aloud) one past regret, mistake, or burden you each want to release this week—whether personal or shared.

Pray together: *"Jesus, we give this to You. We release it into Your hands. We choose forgiveness, healing, and freedom. Make us new."*

If writing, you may symbolically tear up the paper or place it in a jar as an act of surrender.

WEEK 13
SEX AS HOLY FIRE—REDISCOVERING THE GIFT OF INTIMACY

MEDITATION SCRIPTURES

"Marriage is honorable among all, and the bed undefiled; but fornicators and adulterers God will judge."—Hebrews 13:4 (NKJV)

"Let him kiss me with the kisses of his mouth— for your love is better than wine."—Song of Songs 1:2 (NKJV)

"Two are better than one, because they have a good reward for their labor... Again, if two lie down together, they will keep warm; but how can one be warm alone?"—Ecclesiastes 4:9, 11 (NASB)

GUIDED MEDITATION ON SCRIPTURE

Sit quietly together, perhaps holding hands or sitting close.

Read the scriptures aloud slowly. Pause between them, letting the words 'honor,' 'love,' 'warmth,' and 'oneness' settle over you.

Reflect silently:

- How have we viewed sexual intimacy in our marriage—as duty, as pressure, as joy, as connection, or something else?
- Where have we lost sight of God's vision for physical intimacy?
- Where might God be inviting us into healing, freedom, or renewed delight?

Stay quietly together, simply present and open before God.

QUOTE FOR TODAY

"The soul is kissed by God in its innermost regions. With interior yearning, grace and all sweetness, it is drawn upwards in such a way that it passionately bursts out in tears of joy."

—*Hildegard of Bingen*

WORD FOR THE WEEK

Sexual intimacy is one of God's most profound and joyful gifts to marriage—yet for many couples, it becomes complicated, painful, or diminished over time. Busyness, body image issues, past wounds, resentment, medical struggles, or simply the routines of life can steal the wonder from this holy fire.

But scripture gives us a vision of sex as more than mere function or obligation. It is a sacrament of oneness, a joyful celebration of love, a healing balm for the body and soul. It is not meant to be driven by performance or comparison, but by affection, tenderness, playfulness, and grace.

For some couples, this week will be a time to simply honor what is already healthy. For others, it will be an invitation to bring old wounds into the light, to have honest conversations, or to seek healing where shame or distance has taken root. God is not embarrassed by your sexuality—He is the One who designed it for delight, connection, and covenantal love.

This week, ask God to help you see your physical union through His eyes. Lay down pressures or expectations. Reconnect with affection, laughter, patience, and presence. Let the holy fire be rekindled—not by force, but by love.

PSALM TO MEDITATE ON

"You have put more joy in my heart than they have when their grain and wine abound."—Psalm 4:7 (ESV)

GUIDED MEDITATION ON THE PSALM

Read Psalm 4 aloud slowly.

Ask together:

- Lord, how can we recover the joy You intend for our marriage—in all areas, including our intimacy?
- What old lies, wounds, or pressures do we need to let go of?

Sit together, inviting God to restore joy, laughter, and connection between you.

DECLARATIONS FOR THE WEEK

We declare:

- ⸾ Our physical intimacy is holy, blessed, and joyful.
- ⸾ We honor one another with tenderness, patience, and love.
- ⸾ We break agreement with shame, fear, or comparison.
- ⸾ God is restoring delight, playfulness, and unity in our marriage.
- ⸾ We are one—spirit, soul, and body—in Christ.

COMMUNION PRAYER

(Prepare bread (or a cracker) and a small cup of juice. Together, hold the bread and pray).

Lord Jesus Christ, we come before You now, humbled and grateful. You are the Bread of Life, the true Manna from heaven. You gave Your body to be broken for us, that we might be made whole—spirit, soul, and body. You poured out Your blood as the cup of the new covenant, that we might be cleansed, forgiven, and reconciled to God.

We pause to remember Your sacrifice. We remember Your wounds, Your love, Your victory. We remember that You carried our sickness, our grief, our sins, and our shame upon Yourself at the cross (see Isaiah 53:4–5). You conquered death, hell, and the grave, and You rose again, so that we might share in Your life.

We confess, Lord, that we need You. We bring before You every place in our lives and marriage where we are weak, divided, hurting, or

burdened. We ask for Your forgiveness for where we have spoken in anger, withheld love, carried resentment, or failed to honor one another. Wash us clean, Jesus—in Your mercy, cover us with Your righteousness.

As we eat this bread, we receive Your healing. Heal our hearts where they are wounded. Heal our minds where they are anxious or tormented. Heal our bodies where they are sick or weak. Heal our marriage where it has been strained or broken. Let the same power that raised You from the dead now flow through us. Jesus, You made us as embodied souls—spirit and flesh woven together. Thank You that You do not divide the sacred from the physical, but You sanctify it all. As we eat this bread, we remember that You gave Your body so we might know healing and wholeness.

(Eat the bread)

As we drink this cup, we renew our covenant with You and with each other. We declare that we are Yours, and You are ours. We belong to You—as individuals and as a couple. Strengthen the bond between us. Let our love be patient, kind, humble, and enduring. Let forgiveness flow freely in our home. Let Your peace reign over our household. Jesus, thank You for Your blood, poured out for forgiveness and new life. As we drink this cup, we receive Your blood—cleansing, forgiving, and renewing every part of our lives, including our marriage bed.

(Drink the cup)

Jesus, fill us with Your Spirit. Unite us in Your love. Draw us deeper into the mystery of union with You—that we may be one as You and the Father are one. Teach us to love one another with Your supernatural love. Teach us to walk in Your ways. Teach us to see our marriage not only as partnership, but as a holy vessel that carries Your glory into this world.

We receive now—with faith and joy—the blessings You have promised. Blessings of peace, healing, provision, restoration, protection, wisdom, and overflowing grace. We stand in agreement, as one, declaring that no weapon formed against us shall prosper. We break every assignment of the enemy against our lives and marriage. We release blessings over our future, over our family, and over the generations to come.

We invite You into our intimacy, Lord. Heal what has been wounded. Bless what has been good. Rekindle what has grown cold. Let our love be a reflection of Your joyful, self-giving love.

Thank You, Jesus. Amen.

FINAL WORD

Sex is not just about bodies—it's about covenant, joy, and the mystery of becoming one. This week, slow down. Hold each other close. Laugh together. Let love, not pressure, lead you into deeper connection.

COUPLES ACTIVITY: "THE AFFECTION CHALLENGE"

Every day this week, share at least one non-sexual act of affection (a long hug, holding hands, an unexpected kiss, a loving note, or playful touch)—not as a lead-up to intimacy, but as pure connection. Notice how these small acts soften the atmosphere between you and open space for joy.

WEEK 14
NAVIGATING SEASONS OF DISTANCE— WHEN APART, YET ONE

MEDITATION SCRIPTURES

"The Lord watch between you and me when we are absent one from another."—Genesis 31:49 (NKJV)

"For I am convinced that neither death, nor life, nor angels, nor principalities, nor things present, nor things to come, nor powers... nor any other created thing will be able to separate us from the love of God, that is in Christ Jesus our Lord."—Romans 8:38–39 (NASB)

"Though we are absent in body, we are present with you in spirit, delighting to see how disciplined you are and how firm your faith in Christ is."—Colossians 2:5 (NIV)

GUIDED MEDITATION ON SCRIPTURE

Sit quietly together or, if physically apart, read this devotion over a call, message, or prayer.

Read the scriptures aloud, slowly. Let the words settle: absent, yet watched over; nothing separates us from love; present in spirit.

Reflect silently:

- ں Are we walking through a season of physical distance (due to work, family, illness, travel) or emotional distance (due to stress, hurt, or weariness)?
- ں How can we hold onto the truth of being "one" even when we are not together?
- ں What does it look like to stay spiritually connected, even across distance?

Take a few deep breaths, inviting God into the space between you.

QUOTE FOR TODAY

"God is nearer to us than our own soul, for He is the ground in whom our soul stands."

—*Julian of Norwich*

WORD FOR THE WEEK

Every marriage will face seasons of distance. Sometimes it's physical—long work hours, travel, health crises, or family responsibilities that pull you apart. Other times, it's emotional—feeling lonely under the same roof, carrying unspoken disappointments, or drifting into separate worlds.

But scripture reminds us that true love is not confined by proximity. Nothing can separate us from the love of God, and when we remain anchored in Him, we can remain anchored to each other, even across miles or in dry seasons. Physical absence does not have to mean emotional disconnection, and emotional distance does not have to be permanent.

Staying one in spirit takes intention: small check-ins, prayers for each other, meaningful messages, forgiveness, and reminders that *"I see you, I'm with you, I choose you."* And when life allows, it takes the humility to close the distance physically—to prioritize time, to rebuild connection, to fight for presence again.

This week, invite God into whatever distance you're facing. Ask Him to be the bridge between you. Trust that He is holding your union, even when you feel stretched. You are still one, because He is the One who holds you.

PSALM TO MEDITATE ON

"Where can I go from Your Spirit? Or where can I flee from Your presence? If I ascend into heaven, You are there… If I dwell in the uttermost parts of the sea, even there Your hand shall lead me, and Your right hand shall hold me."—Psalm 139:7–10 (NKJV)

GUIDED MEDITATION ON THE PSALM

Read Psalm 139 aloud slowly.

Ask together (or individually, if apart):

- Lord, where do we feel most apart or disconnected?
- How can we invite Your presence into that space?

Picture God's hand gently holding both of you, drawing you closer to Him and to each other.

DECLARATIONS FOR THE WEEK

We declare:

- ও No distance can separate us from God's love or from each other.
- ও We are one in spirit, even when we are apart.
- ও We will stay connected through love, prayer, and intention.
- ও God is the bridge between us, strengthening our bond.
- ও Our love endures all seasons and draws its strength from Christ.

COMMUNION PRAYER

(Prepare bread (or a cracker) and a small cup of juice. Together, hold the bread and pray).

Lord Jesus Christ, we come before You now, humbled and grateful. You are the Bread of Life, the true Manna from heaven. You gave Your body to be broken for us, that we might be made whole—spirit, soul, and body. You poured out Your blood as the cup of the new covenant, that we might be cleansed, forgiven, and reconciled to God.

We pause to remember Your sacrifice. We remember Your wounds, Your love, Your victory. We remember that You carried our sickness, our grief, our sins, and our shame upon Yourself at the cross (see

Isaiah 53:4–5). You conquered death, hell, and the grave, and You rose again, so that we might share in Your life.

We confess, Lord, that we need You. We bring before You every place in our lives and marriage where we are weak, divided, hurting, or burdened. We ask for Your forgiveness for where we have spoken in anger, withheld love, carried resentment, or failed to honor one another. Wash us clean, Jesus—in Your mercy, cover us with Your righteousness.

As we eat this bread, we receive Your healing. Heal our hearts where they are wounded. Heal our minds where they are anxious or tormented. Heal our bodies where they are sick or weak. Heal our marriage where it has been strained or broken. Let the same power that raised You from the dead now flow through us. Jesus, You stretched out Your arms on the cross to close the distance between God and humanity. You understand separation, and You know how to heal it. As we eat this bread, we remember that You have made us one body.

(Eat the bread)

As we drink this cup, we renew our covenant with You and with each other. We declare that we are Yours, and You are ours. We belong to You—as individuals and as a couple. Strengthen the bond between us. Let our love be patient, kind, humble, and enduring. Let forgiveness flow freely in our home. Let Your peace reign over our household. Jesus, thank You for Your blood, poured out for forgiveness and new life. As we drink this cup, we remember that nothing can separate us from Your love—or from the love You have given us for each other.

(Drink the cup)

Jesus, fill us with Your Spirit. Unite us in Your love. Draw us deeper into the mystery of union with You—that we may be one as You and the Father are one. Teach us to love one another with Your supernatural love. Teach us to walk in Your ways. Teach us to see our marriage not only as partnership, but as a holy vessel that carries Your glory into this world.

We receive now—with faith and joy—the blessings You have promised. Blessings of peace, healing, provision, restoration, protection, wisdom, and overflowing grace. We stand in agreement, as one, declaring that no weapon formed against us shall prosper. We break every assignment of the enemy against our lives and marriage. We release blessings over our future, over our family, and over the generations to come.

Be near to us, Lord, in every mile, every moment, and every silence. Teach us how to love well, whether near or far. Knit our hearts together by Your Spirit.

Thank You, Jesus. Amen.

FINAL WORD

Distance will test you, but it can also refine you. Let it become a season of deeper trust, tender longing, and creative love. You are not alone—God is holding you both, and His love knows no distance.

COUPLES ACTIVITY: "BRIDGE THE DISTANCE"

If apart: Send each other a daily message of love or prayer this week, not about logistics or stress, but about connection (for example, *"I'm praying for you today,"* *"I miss you,"* *"I love you, and I'm with you in spirit"*).

If together but feeling distant: Choose one small act each day to close the gap—a long hug, a shared meal without distractions, a handwritten note, or a walk together. End each day by praying (even a short prayer) as one.

WEEK 15
WALKING THROUGH SICKNESS—
TENDERNESS IN TRIALS

MEDITATION SCRIPTURES

"Bear one another's burdens, and so fulfill the law of Christ."—Galatians 6:2 (NKJV)

"Even to your old age, I am He, and even to gray hairs I will carry you! I have made, and I will bear; even I will carry, and will deliver you."—Isaiah 46:4 (NKJV)

"He gives power to the weak, and to those who have no might He increases strength."—Isaiah 40:29 (NKJV)

GUIDED MEDITATION ON SCRIPTURE

Sit quietly together. Take a deep, slow breath.

Read the scriptures aloud, slowly, pausing between each. Let the words rest over you: *bear one another's burdens... I will carry you... power to the weak.*

Reflect silently:

- ڛ How has sickness—physical, emotional, or mental—touched our marriage?
- ڛ How have we learned to care for each other in weakness, or where do we need God's help to love better?
- ڛ What burdens are we carrying alone that God wants to help us carry together?

Sit for a few minutes, inviting the Holy Spirit to pour fresh tenderness into your hearts.

QUOTE FOR TODAY

"Nothing can separate us from the love of Christ; this is the foundation for patient endurance in all trials."

—*Thomas à Kempis*

WORD FOR THE WEEK

Sickness is one of the hardest tests of love because it strips away the easy joys and demands something deeper: presence, patience, endurance, and sacrifice. Whether it's a brief illness, a chronic condition, or emotional or mental health struggles, sickness confronts us with our limits and invites us into Christ-like tenderness.

The world teaches us to value people for their strength, productivity, or what they can give. But the kingdom of God reveals love at its purest when it shows up in weakness—in the gentle touch, the whispered prayer, the hand held through pain, the willingness to serve without reward. This is holy ground.

If you are the one who is sick, remember: you are not a burden; you are beloved. Allow your spouse to love you, and allow God to carry you both. If you are the caregiver, remember: you are not alone. Let God pour His strength into you, and don't neglect your own soul as you serve.

This week, do not rush to "fix" or escape what hurts. Invite God into it. Let sickness become a place of communion, where His love is revealed in the quiet, humble acts of care and presence. Love does not disappear in sickness—it deepens.

PSALM TO MEDITATE ON

"The Lord sustains them on their sickbed and restores them from their bed of illness."—Psalm 41:3 (NIV)

GUIDED MEDITATION ON THE PSALM

Read Psalm 41:3 slowly and gently.

Ask together:

- Lord, where do we need Your sustaining strength right now?
- How can we offer one another comfort and tenderness this week?

Sit in stillness, picturing God gently holding you both—the one who is weak and the one who is helping.

DECLARATIONS FOR THE WEEK

We declare:

- ﺹ God is with us in sickness and in health.
- ﺹ We are not alone; we are upheld by His strength and love.
- ﺹ Our marriage is a place of tenderness, patience, and compassion.
- ﺹ We receive God's healing, whether through miracle or through the daily grace to endure.
- ﺹ Love is being perfected in us, even through trials.

COMMUNION PRAYER

(Prepare bread (or a cracker) and a small cup of juice. Together, hold the bread and pray).

Lord Jesus Christ, we come before You now, humbled and grateful. You are the Bread of Life, the true Manna from heaven. You gave Your body to be broken for us, that we might be made whole—spirit, soul, and body. You poured out Your blood as the cup of the new covenant, that we might be cleansed, forgiven, and reconciled to God.

We pause to remember Your sacrifice. We remember Your wounds, Your love, Your victory. We remember that You carried our sickness, our grief, our sins, and our shame upon Yourself at the cross (see

Isaiah 53:4–5). You conquered death, hell, and the grave, and You rose again, so that we might share in Your life.

We confess, Lord, that we need You. We bring before You every place in our lives and marriage where we are weak, divided, hurting, or burdened. We ask for Your forgiveness for where we have spoken in anger, withheld love, carried resentment, or failed to honor one another. Wash us clean, Jesus—in Your mercy, cover us with Your righteousness.

As we eat this bread, we receive Your healing. Heal our hearts where they are wounded. Heal our minds where they are anxious or tormented. Heal our bodies where they are sick or weak. Heal our marriage where it has been strained or broken. Let the same power that raised You from the dead now flow through us. Jesus, You carried our sickness, our sorrow, and our weakness to the cross. You are our healer, our comforter, and our ever-present help. As we eat this bread, we receive Your broken body—broken so we might be made whole.

(Eat the bread)

As we drink this cup, we renew our covenant with You and with each other. We declare that we are Yours, and You are ours. We belong to You—as individuals and as a couple. Strengthen the bond between us. Let our love be patient, kind, humble, and enduring. Let forgiveness flow freely in our home. Let Your peace reign over our household. Jesus, thank You for Your blood, poured out for forgiveness and new life. As we drink this cup, we receive Your blood—poured out to bring life, forgiveness, and restoration.

(Drink the cup)

Jesus, fill us with Your Spirit. Unite us in Your love. Draw us deeper into the mystery of union with You—that we may be one as You and the Father are one. Teach us to love one another with Your supernatural love. Teach us to walk in Your ways. Teach us to see our marriage not only as partnership, but as a holy vessel that carries Your glory into this world.

We receive now—with faith and joy—the blessings You have promised. Blessings of peace, healing, provision, restoration, protection, wisdom, and overflowing grace. We stand in agreement, as one, declaring that no weapon formed against us shall prosper. We break every assignment of the enemy against our lives and marriage. We release blessings over our future, over our family, and over the generations to come.

We bring our pain, our weariness, and our fear to You. Fill our home with Your peace. Strengthen the one who is ill. Strengthen the one who is caring. Heal where You will, and sustain where we must walk through.

Thank You, Jesus, for being with us in every season. Amen.

FINAL WORD

Sickness is not the end of love; it is the place where love is refined. Let this week be marked not by frustration or fear, but by gentleness, presence, and the quiet strength that only comes from God.

COUPLES ACTIVITY: "COMFORT EXCHANGE"

Each day this week, offer one simple act of comfort or encouragement: a warm drink, a gentle touch, a kind word, a shared prayer, or a moment of quiet together. If one is sick, let the other serve without guilt. If both are weary, lean into God together. End each day whispering, *"We are not alone. God is carrying us."*

WEEK 16
GRIEVING TOGETHER—LOSS, LOVE, AND GOD'S COMFORT

MEDITATION SCRIPTURES

"The Lord is close to the brokenhearted; He saves those who are crushed in spirit."—Psalm 34:18 (NIV)

"Blessed are those who mourn, for they will be comforted."—Matthew 5:4 (NKJV)

"He will wipe every tear from their eyes, and there will be no more death or sorrow or crying or pain. All these things are gone forever."—Revelation 21:4 (NLT)

GUIDED MEDITATION ON SCRIPTURE

Sit together quietly, maybe holding hands or simply sitting near.

Read the scriptures aloud slowly. Pause after each one. Let the words *close to the brokenhearted... blessed are those who mourn... no more sorrow* wash over you.

Reflect silently:

- ﺱ What losses have we walked through—together or individually—that still touch our hearts?
- ﺱ Where have we allowed grief to draw us closer, and where has it built walls?
- ﺱ Where do we need to invite God's comfort into our sorrow, even now?

Let the quiet be a space where no words are needed—just presence.

QUOTE FOR TODAY

"Do not fear the desert of grief. It is there you will find God's deepest well."

—*John of the Cross*

WORD FOR THE WEEK

Grief is a sacred journey, but it is also a lonely one, and even in marriage, two people can grieve the same loss in very different ways. One may want to talk; the other may need silence. One may weep openly; the other may carry sorrow inward. The challenge and gift of grief in marriage is learning to give each other room, while also choosing to walk together.

God does not rush grief. He does not tell us to "move on" or "be strong." Instead, He draws near, holds us in our brokenness, and reminds us that every tear is precious to Him. Scripture promises not only present comfort but also the ultimate healing to come: one day, no more death, no more crying, no more pain.

As a couple, grief can either isolate or deepen intimacy. When you share memories, hold each other's pain, and grieve honestly—without judgment or fixing—you create a space where love becomes a healing balm. And when you invite God into that space, you find a comfort the world cannot give.

This week, honor the grief you carry. Let it be a place where you meet each other tenderly and where you meet God intimately. You do not have to grieve perfectly—you only have to grieve together.

PSALM TO MEDITATE ON

"You keep track of all my sorrows. You have collected all my tears in Your bottle. You have recorded each one in Your book."—Psalm 56:8 (NLT)

GUIDED MEDITATION ON THE PSALM

Read Psalm 56:8 aloud slowly.

Ask together:

- Lord, what grief have we been holding alone that You want to help us carry together?
- How can we make space this week to remember, to honor, and to heal?

Picture God gently collecting your tears—not one is wasted, not one unseen.

DECLARATIONS FOR THE WEEK

We declare:

— God is near to us in grief and holds us in His love.
— Our tears are sacred and seen by God.
— We honor the memories and the love that shaped us.
— We grieve together, not alone.
— We open our hearts to God's comfort, now and forever.

COMMUNION PRAYER

(Prepare bread (or a cracker) and a small cup of juice. Together, hold the bread and pray).

Lord Jesus Christ, we come before You now, humbled and grateful. You are the Bread of Life, the true Manna from heaven. You gave Your body to be broken for us, that we might be made whole—spirit, soul, and body. You poured out Your blood as the cup of the new covenant, that we might be cleansed, forgiven, and reconciled to God.

We pause to remember Your sacrifice. We remember Your wounds, Your love, Your victory. We remember that You carried our sickness, our grief, our sins, and our shame upon Yourself at the cross (see Isaiah 53:4–5). You conquered death, hell, and the grave, and You rose again, so that we might share in Your life.

We confess, Lord, that we need You. We bring before You every place in our lives and marriage where we are weak, divided, hurting, or burdened. We ask for Your forgiveness for where we have spoken in anger, withheld love, carried resentment, or failed to honor one another. Wash us clean, Jesus—in Your mercy, cover us with Your righteousness.

As we eat this bread, we receive Your healing. Heal our hearts where they are wounded. Heal our minds where they are anxious or tormented. Heal our bodies where they are sick or weak. Heal our marriage where it has been strained or broken. Let the same power that raised You from the dead now flow through us. Jesus, You were a man of sorrows, acquainted with grief. You know our loss. You know our tears. You wept at the grave of a friend. You understand. As we eat this bread, we remember Your body—broken, so we might find healing.

(Eat the bread)

As we drink this cup, we renew our covenant with You and with each other. We declare that we are Yours, and You are ours. We belong to You—as individuals and as a couple. Strengthen the bond between us. Let our love be patient, kind, humble, and enduring. Let forgiveness flow freely in our home. Let Your peace reign over our household. Jesus, thank You for Your blood, poured out for forgiveness and new life. As we drink this cup, we remember Your blood—poured out, so we might have hope beyond death.

(Drink the cup)

Jesus, fill us with Your Spirit. Unite us in Your love. Draw us deeper into the mystery of union with You—that we may be one as You and the Father are one. Teach us to love one another with Your supernatural love. Teach us to walk in Your ways. Teach us to see our marriage not only as partnership, but as a holy vessel that carries Your glory into this world.

We receive now—with faith and joy—the blessings You have promised. Blessings of peace, healing, provision, restoration, protection, wisdom, and overflowing grace. We stand in agreement, as one, declaring that no weapon formed against us shall prosper. We break every assignment of the enemy against our lives and marriage. We release blessing over our future, over our family, and over the generations to come.

We bring our grief to You. We bring the names, the memories, the empty spaces. Hold them, Lord. Hold us. Heal us, gently, over time. Fill our home with the light of Your eternal hope.

Thank You, Jesus. Amen.

FINAL WORD

Grief is not something to "get over." It is something to carry and God promises to help you carry it. Let sorrow deepen your love, not diminish it. Let it open your hearts to one another and to the comfort only God can give.

COUPLES ACTIVITY: "REMEMBER, RELEASE, RECEIVE"

Take 20–30 minutes this week to sit together and share:

- One memory of the person or loss you are grieving.
- One feeling or burden you want to release into God's hands.
- One hope or prayer you want to receive for the future.

Pray together, thanking God for the gift of love, the permission to grieve, and the promise of healing.

WEEK 17
BALANCING CHURCH, MINISTRY, AND MARRIAGE

MEDITATION SCRIPTURES

"And whatever you do, whether in word or deed, do it all in the name of the Lord Jesus, giving thanks to God the Father through Him."—Colossians 3:17 (NIV)

"But I have this against you, that you have left your first love."—Revelation 2:4 (NASB)

"Come to Me, all you who labor and are heavy laden, and I will give you rest."—Matthew 11:28 (NKJV)

GUIDED MEDITATION ON SCRIPTURE

Sit together quietly, take a few deep breaths.

Read the scriptures aloud slowly, pausing between each. Let the words settle: *do it all in Jesus' name… first love… come to Me and rest.*

Reflect silently:

- ꙅ How has serving in church or ministry affected our marriage—both positively and negatively?

- ꙅ Where have we felt stretched thin, disconnected, or exhausted in the name of doing good?
- ꙅ What would it look like to prioritize our marriage without neglecting God's call on our lives?

Breathe together in stillness, asking the Holy Spirit to gently show you where adjustments are needed.

QUOTE FOR TODAY

"We must be emptied of what we have, if we are to be filled with what we lack."

—*Meister Eckhart*

WORD FOR THE WEEK

Ministry is a gift and a calling, but it can also quietly erode the foundation of a marriage if it's not held with wisdom and balance. Many couples give and serve and pour themselves out—at church, in leadership, in community—and over time find themselves exhausted, disconnected, or even resentful.

Jesus warned the church at Ephesus: **"You have left your first love."** This was not just about abandoning faith; it was about drifting from what matters most. In marriage, our first ministry is not to the pulpit, the platform, or the people—it is to the one God has given us to love, serve, and walk alongside every day.

This does not mean abandoning ministry; it means integrating it wisely. It means serving together when possible, setting healthy boundaries, protecting time to rest and connect, and regularly checking in: *"Are we okay? Are we thriving? Are we still in love?"* Ministry offered from an empty, neglected marriage does not glorify God; it depletes both partners.

This week, invite God to help you evaluate where you are. Celebrate where ministry has strengthened you. Confess where it has drained or divided you. And commit together to serve from a place of love, unity, and grace—not striving or pressure.

PSALM TO MEDITATE ON

"Unless the Lord builds the house, they labor in vain who build it; unless the Lord guards the city, the watchman stays awake in vain."—Psalm 127:1 (NKJV)

GUIDED MEDITATION ON THE PSALM

Read Psalm 127:1 aloud slowly.

Ask together:

- ﻭ Lord, where have we been laboring in vain—working harder but growing thinner?
- ﻭ How can we let You build and sustain both our marriage and our ministry?

Sit quietly, picturing God gently taking the burden off your shoulders.

DECLARATIONS FOR THE WEEK

We declare:

- ७ Our marriage is our first ministry and our sacred trust.
- ७ We serve joyfully, but not at the expense of our love or health.
- ७ God builds our home and our ministry—we do not carry it alone.
- ७ We are united, strong, and refreshed in Christ.
- ७ We rest, reconnect, and serve from a place of love.

COMMUNION PRAYER

(Prepare bread (or a cracker) and a small cup of juice. Together, hold the bread and pray).

Lord Jesus Christ, we come before You now, humbled and grateful. You are the Bread of Life, the true Manna from heaven. You gave Your body to be broken for us, that we might be made whole—spirit, soul, and body. You poured out Your blood as the cup of the new covenant, that we might be cleansed, forgiven, and reconciled to God.

We pause to remember Your sacrifice. We remember Your wounds, Your love, Your victory. We remember that You carried our sickness, our grief, our sins, and our shame upon Yourself at the cross (see Isaiah 53:4–5). You conquered death, hell, and the grave, and You rose again, so that we might share in Your life.

We confess, Lord, that we need You. We bring before You every place in our lives and marriage where we are weak, divided, hurting, or burdened. We ask for Your forgiveness for where we have spoken in anger, withheld love, carried resentment, or failed to honor one another. Wash us clean, Jesus—in Your mercy, cover us with Your righteousness.

As we eat this bread, we receive Your healing. Heal our hearts where they are wounded. Heal our minds where they are anxious or tormented. Heal our bodies where they are sick or weak. Heal our marriage where it has been strained or broken. Let the same power that raised You from the dead now flow through us. Jesus, You are our first love. You are the reason we serve, the strength we rely on, and the peace we long for. As we eat this bread, we remember Your body— broken, so we could live whole.

(Eat the bread)

As we drink this cup, we renew our covenant with You and with each other. We declare that we are Yours, and You are ours. We belong to You—as individuals and as a couple. Strengthen the bond between us. Let our love be patient, kind, humble, and enduring. Let forgiveness flow freely in our home. Let Your peace reign over our household. Jesus, thank You for Your blood, poured out for forgiveness and new life. As we drink this cup, we receive Your blood—poured out, so we could rest in Your love.

(Drink the cup)

Jesus, fill us with Your Spirit. Unite us in Your love. Draw us deeper into the mystery of union with You—that we may be one as You and the Father are one. Teach us to love one another with Your supernatural love. Teach us to walk in Your ways. Teach us to see our marriage not only as partnership, but as a holy vessel that carries Your glory into this world.

We receive now—with faith and joy—the blessings You have promised. Blessings of peace, healing, provision, restoration, protection, wisdom, and overflowing grace. We stand in agreement, as one, declaring that no weapon formed against us shall prosper. We break every assignment of the enemy against our lives and marriage. We release blessing over our future, over our family, and over the generations to come.

We bring our marriage, our ministry, and our busy hearts before You. Renew our love. Re-center our focus. Teach us to serve You and each other with joy, wisdom, and grace.

Thank You, Jesus. Amen.

FINAL WORD

God never asks you to sacrifice your marriage on the altar of ministry. Let your love be the overflow, not the casualty, of your service. Love well. Serve wisely. Keep Him—and each other—at the center.

COUPLES ACTIVITY: "MARRIAGE CHECK-IN"

Set aside 30–60 minutes this week to check in on these questions:

- What do we love about serving together or separately?
- Where do we feel stretched or strained?
- What boundaries or rhythms could help us protect our marriage?

Pray together, asking God to bless your home as your first ministry.

WEEK 18
PARENTING TOGETHER—UNITED FRONT, TENDER HEARTS

MEDITATION SCRIPTURES

"Train up a child in the way he should go, and when he is old he will not depart from it."—Proverbs 22:6 (NKJV)

"Fathers, do not provoke your children to anger, but bring them up in the discipline and instruction of the Lord."—Ephesians 6:4 (NASB)

"Like arrows in the hand of a warrior, so are the children of one's youth. Blessed is the man whose quiver is full of them."—Psalm 127:4–5 (NKJV)

GUIDED MEDITATION ON SCRIPTURE

Sit together quietly. Take a few deep breaths and settle your hearts.

Read the scriptures aloud slowly, pausing between each. Let the words *train up... do not provoke... arrows in a warrior's hand* settle into your spirit.

Reflect silently:

- ﺱ Where have we been united and strong as parents?
- ﺱ Where have we felt divided, stressed, or unsure?
- ﺱ Where do we need God's wisdom, grace, and strength as we parent (or grandparent, or spiritually parent) right now?

Sit in the quiet, inviting God to show you one simple way to grow stronger together.

QUOTE FOR TODAY

"You are rewarded not according to your work or your time, but according to the measure of your love."

—*St. Catherine of Siena*

WORD FOR THE WEEK

Parenting is both one of the greatest joys and one of the greatest pressures a couple can carry. It stretches your patience, tests your unity, and exposes your weaknesses, but it also gives you daily opportunities to practice love, grace, and teamwork.

Children do not need perfect parents. They need parents who love each other, who admit when they are wrong, and who create an atmosphere of safety and consistency. They need to see a united front—even when decisions are hard—and they need to see tenderness, not just discipline, shaping the home.

But many couples find themselves divided: one too soft, the other too strict; one disengaged, the other overwhelmed; one fearful, the other dismissive. The gift of parenting together is that you get to balance and complement one another, and when you invite God into that process, you gain wisdom and strength beyond your own.

This week, ask God to help you walk in unity and tenderness. Whether you are raising toddlers, teenagers, adults, or spiritual sons and daughters, let your home be a place where love is the loudest voice and grace shapes the atmosphere.

PSALM TO MEDITATE ON

"He will tend His flock like a shepherd; He will gather the lambs in His arms; He will carry them in His bosom, and gently lead those that are with young."—Isaiah 40:11 (ESV)

GUIDED MEDITATION ON THE PSALM

Read Isaiah 40 aloud slowly.

Ask together:

- ꙩ Lord, where do we need Your gentle leadership as we raise, guide, or care for children?
- ꙩ How can we reflect Your shepherd heart to the ones You've entrusted to us?

Picture God gently leading you both, carrying the burdens you feel and the children you love.

DECLARATIONS FOR THE WEEK

We declare:

- ک We are united as parents, guided by God's love and wisdom.
- ک We balance tenderness and strength as we raise those entrusted to us.
- ک God gives us grace to cover our mistakes and wisdom to walk forward.
- ک Our home is a place of love, safety, and blessing.
- ک We trust God with our children's past, present, and future.

COMMUNION PRAYER

(Prepare bread (or a cracker) and a small cup of juice. Together, hold the bread and pray).

Lord Jesus Christ, we come before You now, humbled and grateful. You are the Bread of Life, the true Manna from heaven. You gave Your body to be broken for us, that we might be made whole—spirit, soul, and body. You poured out Your blood as the cup of the new covenant, that we might be cleansed, forgiven, and reconciled to God.

We pause to remember Your sacrifice. We remember Your wounds, Your love, Your victory. We remember that You carried our sickness, our grief, our sins, and our shame upon Yourself at the cross (see Isaiah 53:4–5). You conquered death, hell, and the grave, and You rose again, so that we might share in Your life.

We confess, Lord, that we need You. We bring before You every place in our lives and marriage where we are weak, divided, hurting, or burdened. We ask for Your forgiveness for where we have spoken in anger, withheld love, carried resentment, or failed to honor one another. Wash us clean, Jesus—in Your mercy, cover us with Your righteousness.

As we eat this bread, we receive Your healing. Heal our hearts where they are wounded. Heal our minds where they are anxious or tormented. Heal our bodies where they are sick or weak. Heal our marriage where it has been strained or broken. Let the same power that raised You from the dead now flow through us. Jesus, You welcomed the little children and blessed them. You are the perfect Shepherd, tender and strong, wise and patient. As we eat this bread, we receive Your body—broken to bring wholeness to our family.

(Eat the bread)

As we drink this cup, we renew our covenant with You and with each other. We declare that we are Yours, and You are ours. We belong to You—as individuals and as a couple. Strengthen the bond between us. Let our love be patient, kind, humble, and enduring. Let forgiveness flow freely in our home. Let Your peace reign over our household. Jesus, thank You for Your blood, poured out for forgiveness and new life. As we drink this cup, we receive Your blood—poured out to cover every failure, every fear, every need.

(Drink the cup)

Jesus, fill us with Your Spirit. Unite us in Your love. Draw us deeper into the mystery of union with You—that we may be one as You and the Father are one. Teach us to love one another with Your supernatural love. Teach us to walk in Your ways. Teach us to see our marriage not only as partnership, but as a holy vessel that carries Your glory into this world.

We receive now—with faith and joy—the blessings You have promised. Blessings of peace, healing, provision, restoration, protection, wisdom, and overflowing grace. We stand in agreement, as one, declaring that no weapon formed against us shall prosper. We break every assignment of the enemy against our lives and marriage. We release blessing over our future, over our family, and over the generations to come.

We dedicate our parenting journey to You, Lord. Help us love well, lead humbly, correct gently, and forgive quickly. Teach us to walk together in unity, raising up a generation that knows You.

Thank You, Jesus. Amen.

FINAL WORD

Parenting will stretch you, humble you, and sometimes exhaust you but it will also teach you to love like Christ: sacrificially, joyfully, and with endless grace. Let God carry you as you carry others.

WEEK 19
FINANCIAL STRAIN AND TRUST—
GOD'S PROVISION IN TIGHT PLACES

MEDITATION SCRIPTURES

"And my God shall supply all your need according to His riches in glory by Christ Jesus."—Philippians 4:19 (NKJV)

"Keep your lives free from the love of money and be content with what you have, because God has said, 'Never will I leave you; never will I forsake you.'"—Hebrews 13:5 (NIV)

"The Lord is my shepherd; I shall not want."—Psalm 23:1 (NKJV)

GUIDED MEDITATION ON SCRIPTURE

Sit together quietly. Take a few deep, calming breaths.

Read the scriptures aloud slowly. Let the words *supply all your need… never will I forsake you… I shall not want* sink deep into your spirit.

Reflect silently:

- ꙅ Where have we been feeling financial pressure, fear, or anxiety?

ى How has this strain affected our marriage—emotionally, practically, or spiritually?

ى What would it look like to trust God together with our needs?

Sit in quiet trust, asking the Holy Spirit to lift the heaviness and fill you both with peace.

QUOTE FOR TODAY

"The riches of God are not measured in gold or silver, but in the peace of a heart that rests in Him."

—*Teresa of Ávila*

WORD FOR THE WEEK

Money pressures can test even the strongest marriages. When bills pile up, work feels uncertain, or unexpected expenses arise, couples often experience stress, tension, and even conflict. One may cope by tightening control; the other by avoiding the topic altogether. Fear, blame, or resentment can quietly grow, not because of the money itself, but because of what it represents: security, control, or provision.

But scripture reminds us that God is our true Provider. This doesn't mean money will magically appear, but it means we are never left to carry these burdens alone. Trusting God with finances is not passive; it involves prayer, stewardship, humility, and often, hard conversations. But it also involves releasing fear and remembering that God's provision is bigger than our paychecks.

As a couple, facing financial strain together can actually strengthen your unity, if you are willing to listen, plan, pray, and surrender as a team. It's not about pretending everything's fine but about saying: *We are on the same side. We will walk through this with faith, wisdom, and love.*

This week, name your financial pressures honestly before God. Pray over them together. Ask for wisdom, creative solutions, and daily provision. And most of all, ask for peace—the kind that comes when you know you are cared for, no matter what.

PSALM TO MEDITATE ON

"The young lions lack and suffer hunger; but those who seek the Lord shall not lack any good thing."—Psalm 34:10 (NKJV)

GUIDED MEDITATION ON THE PSALM

Read Psalm 34:10 aloud slowly.

Ask together:

- Lord, where have we been striving in fear instead of trusting You?
- What does "not lack any good thing" look like in this season for us?

Sit quietly, picturing God's open hand stretched toward you, holding what you need—perhaps in ways you didn't expect.

DECLARATIONS FOR THE WEEK

We declare:

- ى God is our Provider, and we trust Him with our needs.
- ى We are united in facing financial pressures together.
- ى We choose peace over fear, wisdom over panic, and love over blame.
- ى God will guide us with creativity, strength, and daily provision.
- ى We are content, grateful, and confident in His care.

COMMUNION PRAYER

(Prepare bread (or a cracker) and a small cup of juice. Together, hold the bread and pray).

Lord Jesus Christ, we come before You now, humbled and grateful. You are the Bread of Life, the true Manna from heaven. You gave Your body to be broken for us, that we might be made whole—spirit, soul, and body. You poured out Your blood as the cup of the new covenant, that we might be cleansed, forgiven, and reconciled to God.

We pause to remember Your sacrifice. We remember Your wounds, Your love, Your victory. We remember that You carried our sickness, our grief, our sins, and our shame upon Yourself at the cross (see Isaiah 53:4–5). You conquered death, hell, and the grave, and You rose again, so that we might share in Your life.

We confess, Lord, that we need You. We bring before You every place in our lives and marriage where we are weak, divided, hurting, or burdened. We ask for Your forgiveness for where we have spoken in anger, withheld love, carried resentment, or failed to honor one another. Wash us clean, Jesus—in Your mercy, cover us with Your righteousness.

As we eat this bread, we receive Your healing. Heal our hearts where they are wounded. Heal our minds where they are anxious or tormented. Heal our bodies where they are sick or weak. Heal our marriage where it has been strained or broken. Let the same power that raised You from the dead now flow through us. Jesus, You multiplied loaves and fish, turned water into wine, and fed Your people manna in the wilderness. You are still the God of provision. As we eat this bread, we remember Your body—given so we could live in freedom, not fear.

(Eat the bread)

As we drink this cup, we renew our covenant with You and with each other. We declare that we are Yours, and You are ours. We belong to You—as individuals and as a couple. Strengthen the bond between us. Let our love be patient, kind, humble, and enduring. Let forgiveness flow freely in our home. Let Your peace reign over our household. Jesus, thank You for Your blood, poured out for forgiveness and new life. As we drink this cup, we receive Your blood—sealing a covenant of love, care, and faithfulness.

(Drink the cup)

Jesus, fill us with Your Spirit. Unite us in Your love. Draw us deeper into the mystery of union with You—that we may be one as You and the Father are one. Teach us to love one another with Your supernatural love. Teach us to walk in Your ways. Teach us to see our marriage not only as partnership, but as a holy vessel that carries Your glory into this world.

We receive now—with faith and joy—the blessings You have promised. Blessings of peace, healing, provision, restoration, protection, wisdom, and overflowing grace. We stand in agreement, as one, declaring that no weapon formed against us shall prosper. We break every assignment of the enemy against our lives and marriage. We release blessing over our future, over our family, and over the generations to come.

We place our finances, our needs, and our fears in Your hands. Help us walk wisely, give generously, steward faithfully, and trust deeply. Remind us that You are our Shepherd; we shall not want.

Thank You, Jesus. Amen.

FINAL WORD

Financial strain may pressure your marriage, but it can also purify your trust—in God and in each other. Let this be a season where you draw closer, not apart. The One who provides for the birds and flowers will not forget you.

COUPLES ACTIVITY: "THE FINANCIAL PEACE CONVERSATION"

Set aside 30–45 minutes this week to:

- ی Name your biggest financial pressures or worries.
- ی Share honestly how it's affecting you emotionally.
- ی Pray together, surrendering your fears.

Identify one small, practical step you can take this week (like making a simple budget, cutting one expense, or seeking counsel).

End by thanking God for what you do have—practicing gratitude shifts the atmosphere.

WEEK 20
DEALING WITH FATIGUE—RESTORING ENERGY, BODY, AND SOUL

MEDITATION SCRIPTURES

"Come to Me, all you who labor and are heavy laden, and I will give you rest."—Matthew 11:28 (NKJV)

"He makes me to lie down in green pastures; He leads me beside the still waters. He restores my soul."—Psalm 23:2–3 (NKJV)

"In returning and rest you shall be saved; in quietness and confidence shall be your strength."—Isaiah 30:15 (NKJV)

GUIDED MEDITATION ON SCRIPTURE

Sit quietly together. Take a few slow, deep breaths—inhale peace, exhale tension.

Read the scriptures aloud, slowly. Let the words *come to Me… He restores… quietness and confidence* wash over your hearts.

Reflect silently:

- Where are we tired—physically, emotionally, relationally, spiritually?

ﺱ How has fatigue been affecting our connection, patience, or joy?

ﺱ What kind of rest or renewal do we need in this season?

Stay quietly in God's presence, allowing Him to refresh you in stillness.

QUOTE FOR TODAY

"We are not saved by our work, but by resting in the arms of God who works within us."

—*Brother Lawrence*

WORD FOR THE WEEK

Marriage, family, work, ministry, health—life pulls from every side, and even the strongest couples will eventually feel weary. But fatigue doesn't just drain the body; it strains the heart. It makes small irritations feel big, intimacy feel like effort, and joy feel out of reach.

The invitation of Jesus is simple yet profound: **Come to Me, and I will give you rest.** This is not just a call to sleep or take a break (though those are important!); it's a call to a deeper rest—the rest of the soul, the rest that comes when we stop striving, when we pause to breathe, pray, connect, and be still.

In marriage, dealing with fatigue means recognizing when you need to slow down together. It means saying, *"We don't have to do everything. We don't have to carry this alone."* It means learning to rest, laugh, and be human again. It may even mean asking for help, releasing some responsibilities, or reprioritizing for a season.

This week, invite God to show you where you are tired and what He wants to restore. Let Him guide you back to green pastures, still waters, and the kind of soul-deep strength that doesn't come from pushing harder but from resting in His care.

PSALM TO MEDITATE ON

"Return to your rest, O my soul, for the Lord has dealt bountifully with you."—Psalm 116:7 (NKJV)

GUIDED MEDITATION ON THE PSALM

Read Psalm 116:7 aloud slowly.

Ask together:

- ی Lord, how are You inviting us to return to rest?
- ی What rhythms or habits can help restore joy and connection?

Picture your souls gently settling into God's peace, like a child resting in a parent's arms.

DECLARATIONS FOR THE WEEK

We declare:

- ی God is restoring our strength, joy, and connection.

- We release striving and receive His peace.
- Our marriage is a place of rest, renewal, and grace.
- We care for our bodies, minds, and spirits as gifts from God.
- We walk this season slowly, gently, together.

COMMUNION PRAYER

(Prepare bread (or a cracker) and a small cup of juice. Together, hold the bread and pray).

Lord Jesus Christ, we come before You now, humbled and grateful. You are the Bread of Life, the true Manna from heaven. You gave Your body to be broken for us, that we might be made whole—spirit, soul, and body. You poured out Your blood as the cup of the new covenant, that we might be cleansed, forgiven, and reconciled to God.

We pause to remember Your sacrifice. We remember Your wounds, Your love, Your victory. We remember that You carried our sickness, our grief, our sins, and our shame upon Yourself at the cross (see Isaiah 53:4–5). You conquered death, hell, and the grave, and You rose again, so that we might share in Your life.

We confess, Lord, that we need You. We bring before You every place in our lives and marriage where we are weak, divided, hurting, or burdened. We ask for Your forgiveness for where we have spoken in anger, withheld love, carried resentment, or failed to honor one another. Wash us clean, Jesus—in Your mercy, cover us with Your righteousness.

As we eat this bread, we receive Your healing. Heal our hearts where they are wounded. Heal our minds where they are anxious or tormented. Heal our bodies where they are sick or weak. Heal our marriage where it has been strained or broken. Let the same power that raised You from the dead now flow through us. Jesus, You worked, You wept, You grew weary—and You also rested in the Father's love. Thank You that You understand our tiredness. As we eat this bread, we receive Your body—broken so we might know wholeness and peace.

(Eat the bread)

As we drink this cup, we renew our covenant with You and with each other. We declare that we are Yours, and You are ours. We belong to You—as individuals and as a couple. Strengthen the bond between us. Let our love be patient, kind, humble, and enduring. Let forgiveness flow freely in our home. Let Your peace reign over our household. Jesus, thank You for Your blood, poured out for forgiveness and new life. As we drink this cup, we receive Your blood—poured out so we might enter the rest of Your finished work.

(Drink the cup)

Jesus, fill us with Your Spirit. Unite us in Your love. Draw us deeper into the mystery of union with You—that we may be one as You and the Father are one. Teach us to love one another with Your supernatural love. Teach us to walk in Your ways. Teach us to see our marriage not only as partnership, but as a holy vessel that carries Your glory into this world.

We receive now—with faith and joy—the blessings You have promised. Blessings of peace, healing, provision, restoration, protection, wisdom, and overflowing grace. We stand in agreement, as one, declaring that no weapon formed against us shall prosper. We break every assignment of the enemy against our lives and marriage. We release blessing over our future, over our family, and over the generations to come.

We lay down our burdens, our exhaustion, and our striving. Breathe new life into us, Lord. Restore our energy, our laughter, our patience, and our love.

Thank You, Jesus. Amen.

FINAL WORD

Rest is not weakness—it is worship. This week, let rest be an act of love: love for God, love for each other, love for the lives you're building together. Slow down, breathe, reconnect—your souls will thank you.

COUPLES ACTIVITY: "THE REST CHECK-IN"

Set aside time to gently ask each other:

- Where do you feel most exhausted right now?
- What helps you feel rested, even in small ways?
- How can I support you this week—practically, emotionally, spiritually?

Then schedule one shared moment of rest: a walk, a meal without distractions, a nap, a shared devotional, or simply time to sit quietly together. Protect it. Make it holy.

COUPLES EXERCISE AND ACTIVITY

"THE REST RESET"

STEP 1: CREATE A REST SPACE

Choose a time this week when you can be alone and undistracted for 30–45 minutes.

Set the space intentionally:

- Light a candle, play soft music, or sit somewhere quiet.
- Put away phones or devices.
- Sit facing each other—maybe holding hands, maybe just close and relaxed.

STEP 2: GENTLE SHARING

Take turns answering these three questions, one at a time:

1. Where am I feeling most tired right now? (Be honest: is it physical, emotional, mental, spiritual, or all the above?)

2. What is one thing that usually helps me feel rested or renewed? (This could be small: a walk, laughter, time with God, a nap, a hug, time outside, music, etc.)

3. What is one thing I long for from you right now to help me feel supported or refreshed? (This could be practical help, a word of encouragement, more time together, more affection, etc.)

Important: While one shares, the other listens without interrupting, correcting, or trying to fix—just listen with your heart.

STEP 3: PRAY OVER EACH OTHER

After both have shared, pray together.

You might pray something like: *"Lord, thank You for the gift of rest. Help us carry each other's burdens with gentleness. Fill our home with peace, joy, and renewal. Teach us to slow down and receive from You and from each other. We give You our tiredness and ask for Your strength. Amen."*

STEP 4: CHOOSE ONE SHARED REST ACTIVITY

Together, pick one thing you will do this week just for rest and connection.

Examples:

- Go for a gentle walk together.

- Share a meal with no phones.
- Take a nap or rest quietly in the same space.
- Watch a movie or read together.
- Have a night of no work or chores—just be together.
- Listen to worship music or pray together.

Keep it simple and doable.

This is not about adding pressure but about opening space for refreshment.

WHY THIS MATTERS

This exercise helps you:

- Name what's weighing on you.
- Listen to each other with empathy.
- Remember you are not alone in your weariness.
- Invite God into your daily rhythms.
- Practice small acts of love that bring life back to your marriage.

DEEPER DISCIPLINES

(confession, fasting, worship, silence, covenant)

WEEK 21
BREAKING GENERATIONAL
PATTERNS—A NEW LEGACY

MEDITATION SCRIPTURES

"Therefore if the Son makes you free, you shall be free indeed."—John 8:36 (NKJV)

"Christ redeemed us from the curse of the law by becoming a curse for us."—Galatians 3:13 (NIV)

"This means that anyone who belongs to Christ has become a new person. The old life is gone; a new life has begun!"—2 Corinthians 5:17 (NLT)

GUIDED MEDITATION ON SCRIPTURE

Sit together quietly, perhaps holding hands or sitting close.

Read the scriptures aloud slowly. Let the words *free indeed... redeemed from the curse... new life has begun* settle into your spirit.

Reflect silently:

- ﺱ What family patterns (spoken or unspoken) have shaped how we love, fight, communicate, or handle stress?

- ى Which of those patterns do we want to leave behind?
- ى What new legacy do we want to build together, by God's grace?

Stay in stillness, asking the Holy Spirit to gently bring clarity, courage, and hope.

QUOTE FOR TODAY

"You may call God love, you may call God goodness. But the best name for God is compassion."

—*Meister Eckhart*

WORD FOR THE WEEK

Every family has patterns—ways of handling conflict, money, affection, pain, faith, fear. Some of these patterns are healthy and life-giving; others are rooted in brokenness, trauma, or sin. Without noticing, we can carry these old patterns into our marriage: shutting down when hurt, controlling when anxious, using harsh words, fearing intimacy, avoiding hard conversations.

The good news of the gospel is that Jesus doesn't just forgive our individual sins; He breaks the power of generational curses. In Him, we are free—free to choose new patterns, free to walk in love, free to become a living picture of His redeeming grace. This is holy, courageous work, and it's part of the legacy you're building together.

Breaking old patterns doesn't happen overnight. It takes honesty, humility, and sometimes help from others (wise counsel, mentors, or therapists). But as you choose forgiveness, new habits, and Spirit-led love, you are planting seeds for the generations after you—your children, your friends, your spiritual sons and daughters—to walk in blessing, not bondage.

This week, ask God to show you one area where He wants to bring freedom. Take hands, pray boldly, and declare: The old ends here. A new legacy begins.

PSALM TO MEDITATE ON

"But the mercy of the Lord is from everlasting to everlasting on those who fear Him, and His righteousness to children's children."—Psalm 103:17 (NKJV)

GUIDED MEDITATION ON THE PSALM

Read Psalm 103 aloud slowly.

Ask together:

- Lord, what mercy are You extending over our family line?
- What do You want to restore or renew in us for the sake of those who come after?

Picture God's mercy flowing down over you, not only for today, but for your children and generations beyond.

DECLARATIONS FOR THE WEEK

We declare:

- In Christ, we are free from every generational curse.
- God's mercy covers our family, past, present, and future.
- We are creating a new legacy of love, faith, and blessing.
- Old patterns end here; new life begins here.
- Our marriage is a testimony of God's redemptive power.

COMMUNION PRAYER

(Prepare bread (or a cracker) and a small cup of juice. Together, hold the bread and pray).

Lord Jesus Christ, we come before You now, humbled and grateful. You are the Bread of Life, the true Manna from heaven. You gave Your body to be broken for us, that we might be made whole—spirit, soul, and body. You poured out Your blood as the cup of the new covenant, that we might be cleansed, forgiven, and reconciled to God.

We pause to remember Your sacrifice. We remember Your wounds, Your love, Your victory. We remember that You carried our sickness, our grief, our sins, and our shame upon Yourself at the cross (see Isaiah 53:4–5). You conquered death, hell, and the grave, and You rose again, so that we might share in Your life.

We confess, Lord, that we need You. We bring before You every place in our lives and marriage where we are weak, divided, hurting, or burdened. We ask for Your forgiveness for where we have spoken in

anger, withheld love, carried resentment, or failed to honor one another. Wash us clean, Jesus—in Your mercy, cover us with Your righteousness.

As we eat this bread, we receive Your healing. Heal our hearts where they are wounded. Heal our minds where they are anxious or tormented. Heal our bodies where they are sick or weak. Heal our marriage where it has been strained or broken. Let the same power that raised You from the dead now flow through us. Jesus, thank You for breaking every chain—sin, shame, addiction, fear, anger, rejection. You bore the curse so we could receive the blessing. As we eat this bread, we remember Your body, broken to make us whole.

(Eat the bread)

As we drink this cup, we renew our covenant with You and with each other. We declare that we are Yours, and You are ours. We belong to You—as individuals and as a couple. Strengthen the bond between us. Let our love be patient, kind, humble, and enduring. Let forgiveness flow freely in our home. Let Your peace reign over our household. Jesus, thank You for Your blood, poured out for forgiveness and new life. As we drink this cup, we receive Your blood, poured out to cleanse us and give us a new inheritance.

(Drink the cup)

Jesus, fill us with Your Spirit. Unite us in Your love. Draw us deeper into the mystery of union with You—that we may be one as You and the Father are one. Teach us to love one another with Your

supernatural love. Teach us to walk in Your ways. Teach us to see our marriage not only as partnership, but as a holy vessel that carries Your glory into this world.

We receive now—with faith and joy—the blessings You have promised. Blessings of peace, healing, provision, restoration, protection, wisdom, and overflowing grace. We stand in agreement, as one, declaring that no weapon formed against us shall prosper. We break every assignment of the enemy against our lives and marriage. We release blessing over our future, over our family, and over the generations to come.

We surrender our family stories to You—the good, the painful, the hidden. Break what needs breaking. Heal what needs healing. Plant in us a new legacy, rooted in Your love.

Thank You, Jesus. Amen.

FINAL WORD

You are not defined by where you come from—you are defined by Whose you are. God specializes in writing new family stories. Let Him write yours.

COUPLES ACTIVITY: "THE LEGACY CONVERSATION"

Set aside time this week to gently talk through:

- What patterns or wounds from our families have impacted us?
- What do we want to carry forward?
- What do we want to leave behind?
- What legacy do we want to create for the next generation?

End by praying: *"Jesus, we give You our family line. Make us agents of blessing, healing, and love."*

WEEK 22
OVERCOMING ADDICTION—
STANDING TOGETHER IN THE FIGHT

MEDITATION SCRIPTURES

"For the Lord your God is the one who goes with you to fight for you against your enemies to give you victory."—Deuteronomy 20:4 (NIV)

"For though a righteous man falls seven times, he rises again."—Proverbs 24:16 (NKJV)

"It is for freedom that Christ has set us free. Stand firm, then, and do not let yourselves be burdened again by a yoke of slavery."—Galatians 5:1 (NIV)

GUIDED MEDITATION ON SCRIPTURE

Sit together quietly. Breathe deeply and slowly.

Read the scriptures aloud, slowly. Let the words *fights for you… rises again… set free* rest over you both.

Reflect silently:

- ی Are we facing (or have we faced) an addiction—whether to substances, pornography, food, work, social media, gambling, anger, control, or anything else?
- ی How has this struggle affected our marriage?
- ی Where do we need God's power, forgiveness, or help—individually or as a couple?

Invite God into the struggle without shame. Just open the door.

QUOTE FOR TODAY

"Do not be satisfied with the little you can do; seek the grace to do what you cannot."

—*St. John of the Cross*

WORD FOR THE WEEK

Addiction thrives in darkness. It isolates, shames, and convinces us we are alone and beyond change. But addiction is not just a personal battle—it impacts marriages deeply: breaking trust, breeding secrecy, fueling resentment, and draining emotional strength. Yet where addiction isolates, God invites connection; where addiction destroys, God rebuilds.

Healing from addiction is rarely a straight line, and it's rarely quick. It takes confession, humility, accountability, often outside help, and above all, grace. For couples, it means learning to be honest without shaming, supportive without controlling, forgiving without enabling.

166

It means remembering that the real enemy is not your spouse—the real enemy is the bondage trying to steal from both of you.

Whether one or both of you struggle, remember: you are on the same side. Christ has already won the victory. You stand under His banner, not in your own strength, but in His. Get the help you need—from counselors, pastors, recovery groups, or trusted friends—and keep your marriage a place of light, not hiding.

This week, choose to name the battle, bring it into the open, and stand together. Addiction is not your identity, and failure is not the end of the story. In Christ, you rise again.

PSALM TO MEDITATE ON

"He brought them out of darkness, the utter darkness, and broke away their chains."—Psalm 107:14 (NIV)

GUIDED MEDITATION ON THE PSALM

Read Psalm 107 aloud slowly.

Ask together:

- ﺱ Lord, where are You inviting us out of darkness into light?
- ﺱ What chains do You want to break in our lives, individually or together?

Picture God breaking chains—not by human strength, but by His grace and love.

DECLARATIONS FOR THE WEEK

We declare:

- ٯ In Christ, we are free from every chain of addiction.
- ٯ We walk in the light, not in hiding.
- ٯ We stand together as a team, not as enemies.
- ٯ We forgive, we support, we rise again by God's grace.
- ٯ Our marriage is a place of healing, courage, and freedom.

COMMUNION PRAYER

**(Prepare bread (or a cracker) and a small cup of juice.
Together, hold the bread and pray).**

Lord Jesus Christ, we come before You now, humbled and grateful. You are the Bread of Life, the true Manna from heaven. You gave Your body to be broken for us, that we might be made whole—spirit, soul, and body. You poured out Your blood as the cup of the new covenant, that we might be cleansed, forgiven, and reconciled to God.

We pause to remember Your sacrifice. We remember Your wounds, Your love, Your victory. We remember that You carried our sickness, our grief, our sins, and our shame upon Yourself at the cross (see Isaiah 53:4–5). You conquered death, hell, and the grave, and You rose again, so that we might share in Your life.

We confess, Lord, that we need You. We bring before You every place in our lives and marriage where we are weak, divided, hurting, or burdened. We ask for Your forgiveness for where we have spoken in

anger, withheld love, carried resentment, or failed to honor one another. Wash us clean, Jesus—in Your mercy, cover us with Your righteousness.

As we eat this bread, we receive Your healing. Heal our hearts where they are wounded. Heal our minds where they are anxious or tormented. Heal our bodies where they are sick or weak. Heal our marriage where it has been strained or broken. Let the same power that raised You from the dead now flow through us. Jesus, You came to set captives free. You took our sin, shame, and bondage to the cross. You broke the power of darkness. As we eat this bread, we receive Your broken body—given to heal, restore, and strengthen us.

(Eat the bread)

As we drink this cup, we renew our covenant with You and with each other. We declare that we are Yours, and You are ours. We belong to You—as individuals and as a couple. Strengthen the bond between us. Let our love be patient, kind, humble, and enduring. Let forgiveness flow freely in our home. Let Your peace reign over our household. Jesus, thank You for Your blood, poured out for forgiveness and new life. As we drink this cup, we receive Your blood—poured out to cleanse us and break every chain.

(Drink the cup)

Jesus, fill us with Your Spirit. Unite us in Your love. Draw us deeper into the mystery of union with You—that we may be one as You and the Father are one. Teach us to love one another with Your

supernatural love. Teach us to walk in Your ways. Teach us to see our marriage not only as partnership, but as a holy vessel that carries Your glory into this world.

We receive now—with faith and joy—the blessings You have promised. Blessings of peace, healing, provision, restoration, protection, wisdom, and overflowing grace. We stand in agreement, as one, declaring that no weapon formed against us shall prosper. We break every assignment of the enemy against our lives and marriage. We release blessing over our future, over our family, and over the generations to come.

We surrender our struggles, our addictions, our past failures into Your hands. We receive Your freedom, Your forgiveness, and Your power. Make our marriage a testimony of Your redemption.

Thank You, Jesus. Amen.

FINAL WORD

Addiction does not have the final say—Jesus does. Step into the light together. Seek help, hold on to hope, and know that every fall is another chance to rise again, stronger and more free.

COUPLES ACTIVITY: "THE BRAVE CONVERSATION"

Set aside time this week to gently, honestly discuss:

- Are there areas of struggle or addiction we need to bring into the light?
- How can we support, not shame, one another?
- What next step—small or big—do we need to take toward healing?

Pray together, asking God for courage, wisdom, and the right help. Then take that next step, even if it's just one small act of honesty.

WEEK 23
THE POWER OF CONFESSION— TRANSPARENCY BEFORE GOD AND EACH OTHER

MEDITATION SCRIPTURES

"Therefore, confess your sins to one another, and pray for one another, that you may be healed. The effective, fervent prayer of a righteous man avails much."—James 5:16 (NKJV)

"If we confess our sins, He is faithful and just to forgive us our sins and to cleanse us from all unrighteousness."—1 John 1:9 (NKJV)

"Search me, O God, and know my heart; test me and know my anxious thoughts."—Psalm 139:23 (NLT)

GUIDED MEDITATION ON SCRIPTURE

Sit quietly together. Take a deep, slow breath.

Read the scriptures aloud, slowly, pausing after each: confess… pray… be healed… forgive… cleanse… search me.

Reflect silently:

- ی Where have I been withholding truth—from God, from my spouse, or even from myself?
- ی What am I afraid to confess—big or small?
- ی What healing or freedom might come if I open up honestly?

Invite God to shine His gentle light on hidden places, not with condemnation, but with love.

QUOTE FOR TODAY

"If you want to reach the heart of God, go to Him with both your hands full of confession and your heart full of love."

—*St. Augustine*

WORD FOR THE WEEK

Confession is not about shame; it's about freedom. It's not about punishment; it's about connection. In marriage, confession breaks the walls that secrecy builds. It says, Here I am, imperfect but willing. Here's my weakness, my failure, my need—not so you can condemn me, but so we can be real, together, before God.

Scripture promises that confession brings healing, not just forgiveness. It heals the soul, softens the heart, and restores intimacy. But many couples avoid it—out of fear, pride, or the belief that hiding will protect the relationship. Yet hidden things grow in power, while confessed things lose their grip.

Confession also invites grace. It reminds us that marriage is not a contract between two perfect people but a covenant between two forgiven people, held together by the mercy of God. When we confess, we open the door for God's love to enter our most tender places.

This week, take a brave step toward transparency. Ask God to help you confess where you've fallen short, not to shame yourself or your spouse, but to open the path to deeper trust, grace, and healing. You are fully known, fully loved, and fully invited to walk in the light.

PSALM TO MEDITATE ON

"Have mercy on me, O God, according to Your lovingkindness; according to the multitude of Your tender mercies, blot out my transgressions."—Psalm 51:1 (NKJV)

GUIDED MEDITATION ON THE PSALM

Read Psalm 51:1 slowly, almost as a whisper.

Ask together:

- Lord, what do You want me to bring into the light?
- How can we create a safe space to confess and forgive each other?

Picture God's mercy washing over you both like gentle rain, cleansing and restoring.

DECLARATIONS FOR THE WEEK

We declare:

- We walk in the light, not in secrecy.
- God's mercy is greater than our mistakes.
- Our marriage is a safe place for truth, grace, and forgiveness.
- We confess, we forgive, we heal—together.
- We are growing in honesty, love, and freedom.

COMMUNION PRAYER

(Prepare bread (or a cracker) and a small cup of juice. Together, hold the bread and pray).

Lord Jesus Christ, we come before You now, humbled and grateful. You are the Bread of Life, the true Manna from heaven. You gave Your body to be broken for us, that we might be made whole—spirit, soul, and body. You poured out Your blood as the cup of the new covenant, that we might be cleansed, forgiven, and reconciled to God.

We pause to remember Your sacrifice. We remember Your wounds, Your love, Your victory. We remember that You carried our sickness, our grief, our sins, and our shame upon Yourself at the cross (see Isaiah 53:4–5). You conquered death, hell, and the grave, and You rose again, so that we might share in Your life.

We confess, Lord, that we need You. We bring before You every place in our lives and marriage where we are weak, divided, hurting, or

burdened. We ask for Your forgiveness for where we have spoken in anger, withheld love, carried resentment, or failed to honor one another. Wash us clean, Jesus—in Your mercy, cover us with Your righteousness.

As we eat this bread, we receive Your healing. Heal our hearts where they are wounded. Heal our minds where they are anxious or tormented. Heal our bodies where they are sick or weak. Heal our marriage where it has been strained or broken. Let the same power that raised You from the dead now flow through us. Jesus, You already know us fully—every weakness, every sin, every hidden place—and yet You love us completely. You came not to condemn, but to save. As we eat this bread, we remember Your body, broken to carry our burdens.

(Eat the bread)

As we drink this cup, we renew our covenant with You and with each other. We declare that we are Yours, and You are ours. We belong to You—as individuals and as a couple. Strengthen the bond between us. Let our love be patient, kind, humble, and enduring. Let forgiveness flow freely in our home. Let Your peace reign over our household. Jesus, thank You for Your blood, poured out for forgiveness and new life. As we drink this cup, we receive Your blood, poured out to cleanse us and make us whole.

(Drink the cup)

Jesus, fill us with Your Spirit. Unite us in Your love. Draw us deeper into the mystery of union with You—that we may be one as You and the Father are one. Teach us to love one another with Your supernatural love. Teach us to walk in Your ways. Teach us to see our marriage not only as partnership, but as a holy vessel that carries Your glory into this world.

We receive now—with faith and joy—the blessings You have promised. Blessings of peace, healing, provision, restoration, protection, wisdom, and overflowing grace. We stand in agreement, as one, declaring that no weapon formed against us shall prosper. We break every assignment of the enemy against our lives and marriage. We release blessing over our future, over our family, and over the generations to come.

We open our hearts to You and to each other. Help us confess with courage, forgive with grace, and love with Your love. Make our marriage a picture of Your mercy.

Thank You, Jesus. Amen.

FINAL WORD

Confession is not the end of the story—it's the beginning of healing. Walk in the light this week, knowing that every step of honesty makes room for deeper love.

COUPLES ACTIVITY: "THE HONESTY HOUR"

Set aside time this week for a gentle, judgment-free conversation:

- ﺱ **Ask each other:** Is there anything on your heart—regret, struggle, frustration, fear—that you want to share?
- ﺱ Listen with open hands and an open heart, without rushing to fix or defend.
- ﺱ Pray together afterward, asking God for healing, forgiveness, and fresh grace.

If something heavy comes up, consider seeking pastoral or professional help to walk through it wisely.

WEEK 24
EMOTIONAL INTIMACY—KNOWING AND BEING KNOWN

MEDITATION SCRIPTURES

"Rejoice with those who rejoice; weep with those who weep."—Romans 12:15 (NKJV)

"Above all, love each other deeply, because love covers over a multitude of sins."—1 Peter 4:8 (NIV)

"As iron sharpens iron, so one person sharpens another."—Proverbs 27:17 (NLT)

GUIDED MEDITATION ON SCRIPTURE

Sit quietly together. Take a slow, deep breath.

Read the scriptures aloud, pausing between each: rejoice… weep… love deeply… sharpen one another.

Reflect silently:

- ꙅ Do I feel truly known by my spouse—in joy, in sorrow, in struggle?

179

- Have I made space to really know them—their fears, hopes, dreams, and wounds?
- Where can we grow in emotional connection this season?

Sit in stillness together, asking God to deepen the space between your hearts.

QUOTE FOR TODAY

"The soul has a longing to be known, not in part but wholly, and it is God alone who knows us thus. Yet in love, we mirror this knowing to each other."

—*Julian of Norwich*

WORD FOR THE WEEK

Emotional intimacy is the heart of marital connection. It's the quiet sense of being seen, understood, and loved, not just for what you do, but for who you are. It's sharing joys without jealousy, wounds without shame, and dreams without fear of dismissal.

Yet emotional intimacy doesn't just happen. Life's demands can crowd it out. Unspoken hurts can harden the heart. We can get stuck in surface conversations—schedules, logistics, small talk—and miss the chance to share what really matters. Over time, we may live side by side, but not heart to heart.

The good news is that emotional intimacy can always be nurtured. It grows in small, intentional moments: listening without fixing, asking thoughtful questions, showing curiosity about each other's inner world, and creating space for vulnerability. It's not about being perfect—it's about being present.

This week, ask God to help you slow down and reconnect at the level of the heart. Whether it's laughter or tears, excitement or fear, let your marriage be a place where both of you can say, I am known, and I am loved.

PSALM TO MEDITATE ON

"O Lord, You have searched me and known me. You know when I sit down and when I rise up; You understand my thought from afar."—Psalm 139:1–2 (NASB)

GUIDED MEDITATION ON THE PSALM

Read Psalm 139:1-2 slowly.

Ask together:

- ﮑ Lord, how can we mirror Your knowing love to one another?
- ﮑ Where do we need to be more open, more gentle, or more attentive?

Picture God smiling over you both—fully knowing you, fully loving you—and inviting you to share that same grace.

DECLARATIONS FOR THE WEEK

We declare:

- ﺱ Our marriage is a safe place for honesty, vulnerability, and love.
- ﺱ We are learning to know and love each other deeply.
- ﺱ We listen, we bless, and we build each other up.
- ﺱ We are fully known by God and fully accepted in Christ.
- ﺱ We are united in heart, growing in emotional intimacy.

COMMUNION PRAYER

(Prepare bread (or a cracker) and a small cup of juice. Together, hold the bread and pray).

Lord Jesus Christ, we come before You now, humbled and grateful. You are the Bread of Life, the true Manna from heaven. You gave Your body to be broken for us, that we might be made whole—spirit, soul, and body. You poured out Your blood as the cup of the new covenant, that we might be cleansed, forgiven, and reconciled to God.

We pause to remember Your sacrifice. We remember Your wounds, Your love, Your victory. We remember that You carried our sickness, our grief, our sins, and our shame upon Yourself at the cross (see Isaiah 53:4–5). You conquered death, hell, and the grave, and You rose again, so that we might share in Your life.

We confess, Lord, that we need You. We bring before You every place in our lives and marriage where we are weak, divided, hurting, or

182

burdened. We ask for Your forgiveness for where we have spoken in anger, withheld love, carried resentment, or failed to honor one another. Wash us clean, Jesus—in Your mercy, cover us with Your righteousness.

As we eat this bread, we receive Your healing. Heal our hearts where they are wounded. Heal our minds where they are anxious or tormented. Heal our bodies where they are sick or weak. Heal our marriage where it has been strained or broken. Let the same power that raised You from the dead now flow through us. Jesus, You know us fully—every thought, every longing, every hurt, every joy. You do not turn away; You draw near. As we eat this bread, we remember Your body, given in love.

(Eat the bread)

As we drink this cup, we renew our covenant with You and with each other. We declare that we are Yours, and You are ours. We belong to You—as individuals and as a couple. Strengthen the bond between us. Let our love be patient, kind, humble, and enduring. Let forgiveness flow freely in our home. Let Your peace reign over our household. Jesus, thank You for Your blood, poured out for forgiveness and new life. As we drink this cup, we receive Your blood, poured out to make us whole.

(Drink the cup)

Jesus, fill us with Your Spirit. Unite us in Your love. Draw us deeper into the mystery of union with You—that we may be one as You and

the Father are one. Teach us to love one another with Your supernatural love. Teach us to walk in Your ways. Teach us to see our marriage not only as partnership, but as a holy vessel that carries Your glory into this world.

We receive now—with faith and joy—the blessings You have promised. Blessings of peace, healing, provision, restoration, protection, wisdom, and overflowing grace. We stand in agreement, as one, declaring that no weapon formed against us shall prosper. We break every assignment of the enemy against our lives and marriage. We release blessing over our future, over our family, and over the generations to come.

Help us, Lord, to know each other as You know us—with patience, tenderness, and grace. Heal old wounds, soften our hearts, and teach us to love at the deepest places.

Thank You, Jesus. Amen.

FINAL WORD

Emotional intimacy is not a luxury—it's a gift and a calling. Slow down this week. Ask, listen, share, laugh, cry. Let your hearts draw close again, and you will find Christ right there in the center.

COUPLES ACTIVITY: "THE HEART CHECK-IN"

Set aside 20–30 minutes this week to ask each other:

ﺱ What has brought you the most joy lately?

- ی What has weighed on your heart?
- ی What's one thing you need from me right now—emotionally or spiritually?

Listen gently. No fixing, no defending. Just presence. End with a simple prayer or hug, thanking God for the gift of knowing and being known.

WEEK 25
CHOOSING JOY—CELEBRATING LIFE TOGETHER

MEDITATION SCRIPTURES

"Rejoice in the Lord always. Again I will say, rejoice!"—Philippians 4:4 (NKJV)

"The Lord your God in your midst, the Mighty One, will save; He will rejoice over you with gladness, He will quiet you with His love, He will rejoice over you with singing."—Zephaniah 3:17 (NKJV)

"A cheerful heart is good medicine, but a crushed spirit dries up the bones."—Proverbs 17:22 (NIV)

GUIDED MEDITATION ON SCRIPTURE

Sit quietly together, maybe holding hands or sitting close.

Read the scriptures aloud slowly. Let the words *rejoice... gladness... singing... cheerful heart* rest over you.

Reflect silently:

    ى What has brought us joy lately—big or small?

ﺱ Where have we forgotten to celebrate or give thanks?

ﺱ How can we cultivate a spirit of joy, even in hard seasons?

Take a few slow breaths, asking God to awaken fresh gratitude and joy in your hearts.

QUOTE FOR TODAY

"The fullness of joy is to behold God in everything."

—*Julian of Norwich*

WORD FOR THE WEEK

Marriage isn't just about surviving challenges—it's about sharing joy. God designed us not only to carry burdens together but to celebrate blessings together: a warm meal, a kind word, a beautiful sunset, a shared laugh, a quiet victory. Yet in the rush of life, we can easily overlook the good and focus only on the hard.

Joy is not the same as pretending everything is fine. Joy is a posture of the heart that says: *Even here, God is good. Even now, there is beauty. Even in this, we can laugh, dance, and give thanks.* Scripture shows us that God Himself rejoices over us—with gladness, with singing! He invites us to echo His joy.

For many couples, joy must be intentional. It's found in slowing down to notice blessings, choosing gratitude over grumbling, creating moments of lightness, and making room for fun. Joy strengthens resilience, heals emotional weariness, and deepens connection. It's not a bonus; it's part of God's design for love.

This week, choose joy—deliberately, creatively, unapologetically. Celebrate small wins. Laugh often. Thank God together for His gifts. Let your home be a place where joy is practiced, protected, and shared.

PSALM TO MEDITATE ON

"You have turned for me my mourning into dancing; You have put off my sackcloth and clothed me with gladness."—Psalm 30:11 (NKJV)

GUIDED MEDITATION ON THE PSALM

Read Psalm 30:11 aloud slowly.

Ask together:

- Lord, where have You already brought us from sorrow into joy?
- How can we dance—literally or spiritually—in gratitude this week?

Picture God lifting heaviness off your shoulders and clothing you both with gladness.

DECLARATIONS FOR THE WEEK

We declare:

- Our marriage is a place of joy, laughter, and celebration.

ꙅ We choose to notice and thank God for His gifts, big and small.

ꙅ We carry joy, even through trials, anchored in God's goodness.

ꙅ We make room for fun, play, and delight together.

ꙅ Our hearts are lifted, our home is lightened, our spirits are renewed.

COMMUNION PRAYER

(Prepare bread (or a cracker) and a small cup of juice. Together, hold the bread and pray).

Lord Jesus Christ, we come before You now, humbled and grateful. You are the Bread of Life, the true Manna from heaven. You gave Your body to be broken for us, that we might be made whole—spirit, soul, and body. You poured out Your blood as the cup of the new covenant, that we might be cleansed, forgiven, and reconciled to God.

We pause to remember Your sacrifice. We remember Your wounds, Your love, Your victory. We remember that You carried our sickness, our grief, our sins, and our shame upon Yourself at the cross (see Isaiah 53:4–5). You conquered death, hell, and the grave, and You rose again, so that we might share in Your life.

We confess, Lord, that we need You. We bring before You every place in our lives and marriage where we are weak, divided, hurting, or burdened. We ask for Your forgiveness for where we have spoken in anger, withheld love, carried resentment, or failed to honor one another. Wash us clean, Jesus—in Your mercy, cover us with Your righteousness.

As we eat this bread, we receive Your healing. Heal our hearts where they are wounded. Heal our minds where they are anxious or tormented. Heal our bodies where they are sick or weak. Heal our marriage where it has been strained or broken. Let the same power that raised You from the dead now flow through us. Jesus, You are the Joy-Giver. You came to bring life—abundant, overflowing, eternal. You rejoiced in the Father, in Your friends, and even in the cross, knowing the joy set before You. As we eat this bread, we remember Your body, broken so we could share in Your life.

(Eat the bread)

As we drink this cup, we renew our covenant with You and with each other. We declare that we are Yours, and You are ours. We belong to You—as individuals and as a couple. Strengthen the bond between us. Let our love be patient, kind, humble, and enduring. Let forgiveness flow freely in our home. Let Your peace reign over our household. Jesus, thank You for Your blood, poured out for forgiveness and new life. As we drink this cup, we receive Your blood, poured out to bring us into the joy of Your love.

(Drink the cup)

Jesus, fill us with Your Spirit. Unite us in Your love. Draw us deeper into the mystery of union with You—that we may be one as You and the Father are one. Teach us to love one another with Your

supernatural love. Teach us to walk in Your ways. Teach us to see our marriage not only as partnership, but as a holy vessel that carries Your glory into this world.

We receive now—with faith and joy—the blessings You have promised. Blessings of peace, healing, provision, restoration, protection, wisdom, and overflowing grace. We stand in agreement, as one, declaring that no weapon formed against us shall prosper. We break every assignment of the enemy against our lives and marriage. We release blessing over our future, over our family, and over the generations to come.

We thank You, Lord, for the blessings we see and the ones we forget. Awaken joy in us again. Teach us to dance in the light of Your love.

Thank You, Jesus. Amen.

FINAL WORD

Joy is a gift and a practice. Make space this week to smile, laugh, play, celebrate, and give thanks. Let your marriage be marked by joy that points to the God who rejoices over you.

COUPLES ACTIVITY: "THE JOY LIST"

Together, make a list of 10 things that bring you joy as a couple—simple, daily pleasures or special memories.

Examples:

- Watching the sunset
- Cooking a favorite meal
- Listening to music
- Walking together
- Telling old funny stories

Then pick one or two and do them this week—intentionally, with no agenda but joy.

WEEK 26
REKINDLING LOVE—RETURNING TO OUR FIRST JOY

MEDITATION SCRIPTURES

"I remember the devotion of your youth, your love as a bride, how you followed Me in the wilderness, in a land not sown."—Jeremiah 2:2 (ESV)

"Nevertheless I have this against you, that you have left your first love. Remember therefore from where you have fallen; repent and do the first works."—Revelation 2:4–5 (NKJV)

"Set me as a seal upon your heart, as a seal upon your arm; for love is strong as death, jealousy as cruel as the grave."—Song of Songs 8:6 (NKJV)

GUIDED MEDITATION ON SCRIPTURE

Sit quietly together, perhaps holding hands or resting close.

Read the scriptures aloud slowly. Let the words *first love… devotion… seal upon your heart… love is strong* soak into you.

Reflect silently:

- ی What was our relationship like in the early days—what drew us together, what made us laugh, what stirred our hearts?
- ی Where have we drifted or grown cold?
- ی What simple steps could help us return to that first love, now with deeper wisdom?

Sit in stillness, inviting God to refresh and renew your love.

QUOTE FOR TODAY

"The soul who loves God finds in Him endless newness, and in that newness, a joy ever rekindled."

—*Teresa of Ávila*

WORD FOR THE WEEK

Every marriage begins with passion, wonder, and hope, but over time, life happens: routines settle in, burdens increase, and familiarity can dull the sparkle. Rekindling love isn't about recreating the past; it's about remembering what matters and choosing to treasure it afresh.

Scripture invites us to return to our "first love"—not with guilt, but with longing. What were the small gestures, the words, the moments that once made your hearts leap? What would it look like to bring some of that tenderness, attention, and intentionality into today?

Rekindling love doesn't mean ignoring wounds or pretending nothing has changed. It means bringing your full selves—healed, humbled, matured—back to a place of delight and devotion. It's choosing to be not just partners, but lovers and friends again.

This week, ask God to breathe fresh wind into your love. Ask Him to remind you why you said "yes"—and to help you keep saying "yes," over and over, every day.

PSALM TO MEDITATE ON

"You have put gladness in my heart, more than in the season that their grain and wine increased."—Psalm 4:7 (NKJV)

GUIDED MEDITATION ON THE PSALM

Read Psalm 4:7 slowly.

Ask together:

- ﺱ Lord, where have we lost gladness in our love?
- ﺱ What are You inviting us to rediscover, reignite, or rejoice in together?

Picture God filling your hearts with new joy, beyond circumstances or routine.

DECLARATIONS FOR THE WEEK

We declare:

- Our love is alive, growing, and worth cherishing.
- We remember the beauty of our beginning and bring that joy into today.
- God is renewing our passion, friendship, and devotion.
- We are lovers, companions, and covenant partners.
- Our hearts are sealed together by God's strong, enduring love.

COMMUNION PRAYER

(Prepare bread (or a cracker) and a small cup of juice. Together, hold the bread and pray).

Lord Jesus Christ, we come before You now, humbled and grateful. You are the Bread of Life, the true Manna from heaven. You gave Your body to be broken for us, that we might be made whole—spirit, soul, and body. You poured out Your blood as the cup of the new covenant, that we might be cleansed, forgiven, and reconciled to God.

We pause to remember Your sacrifice. We remember Your wounds, Your love, Your victory. We remember that You carried our sickness, our grief, our sins, and our shame upon Yourself at the cross (see Isaiah 53:4–5). You conquered death, hell, and the grave, and You rose again, so that we might share in Your life.

We confess, Lord, that we need You. We bring before You every place in our lives and marriage where we are weak, divided, hurting, or burdened. We ask for Your forgiveness for where we have spoken in anger, withheld love, carried resentment, or failed to honor one another. Wash us clean, Jesus—in Your mercy, cover us with Your righteousness.

As we eat this bread, we receive Your healing. Heal our hearts where they are wounded. Heal our minds where they are anxious or tormented. Heal our bodies where they are sick or weak. Heal our marriage where it has been strained or broken. Let the same power that raised You from the dead now flow through us. Jesus, You are the Bridegroom of our souls—always pursuing, always delighting, always faithful. Thank You for showing us what covenant love looks like. As we eat this bread, we remember Your body—given for love.

(Eat the bread)

As we drink this cup, we renew our covenant with You and with each other. We declare that we are Yours, and You are ours. We belong to You—as individuals and as a couple. Strengthen the bond between us. Let our love be patient, kind, humble, and enduring. Let forgiveness flow freely in our home. Let Your peace reign over our household. Jesus, thank You for Your blood, poured out for forgiveness and new life. As we drink this cup, we receive Your blood—poured out to make us one with You and with each other.

(Drink the cup)

Jesus, fill us with Your Spirit. Unite us in Your love. Draw us deeper into the mystery of union with You—that we may be one as You and the Father are one. Teach us to love one another with Your supernatural love. Teach us to walk in Your ways. Teach us to see our marriage not only as partnership, but as a holy vessel that carries Your glory into this world.

We receive now—with faith and joy—the blessings You have promised. Blessings of peace, healing, provision, restoration, protection, wisdom, and overflowing grace. We stand in agreement, as one, declaring that no weapon formed against us shall prosper. We break every assignment of the enemy against our lives and marriage. We release blessing over our future, over our family, and over the generations to come.

We ask You to rekindle what has cooled, to heal what has been hurt, to reignite what has dimmed. Make our love fresh, playful, tender, and strong. Help us keep choosing each other, every day.

Thank You, Jesus. Amen.

FINAL WORD

Love that lasts is love that renews. Let this week be a time to rediscover, refresh, and rejoice in the gift you have in each other—not as you once were, but as you are now, in grace.

COUPLES ACTIVITY: "FIRST LOVE REMINDERS"

This week, each of you do two things:

1. Share one memory from your early days that still makes you smile or feel warm toward each other.
2. Choose one small act to "recreate" or "reimagine"—like a favorite meal, place, song, or activity you used to enjoy.

Finish by praying: *"Lord, thank You for bringing us together. Help us never take this love for granted. Renew us, strengthen us, and let joy rise again."*

HALFWAY MARK ENCOURAGEMENT

WEEK 26 MILESTONE

Dear Beloved Couple,

You've reached the halfway point in this 52-week devotional journey—pause for a moment and breathe that in.

Fifty-two weeks was never about perfection. It's about showing up, week after week, as two people committed to love, learning, and growing—even when it's messy, even when it's hard, even when you miss a week and come back again.

If you've made it here, it means you have been planting seeds—seeds of hope, forgiveness, joy, honesty, prayer, and tenderness. And maybe you haven't seen all the fruit yet. Maybe some weeks have felt dry or routine. That's okay. Faithfulness bears quiet fruit before it bears visible fruit.

Let this halfway moment remind you: God is with you. He sees every effort, every quiet prayer, every small act of love you offer each other. And He delights in it. You are not walking this path alone—He is building something beautiful with you.

SHORT EXHORTATION

"And let us not grow weary while doing good, for in due season we shall reap if we do not lose heart."—Galatians 6:9 (NKJV)

Keep going. Keep showing up. Keep sowing love, even in small, imperfect ways.

Marriage is not a straight path—it's a winding road with hills, valleys, laughter, sorrow, growth, and grace. The couples who flourish are not those who never struggle, but those who keep returning to each other and to God.

Do not lose heart. There is a harvest coming—a deeper love, a stronger unity, a sweeter joy. Keep walking toward it, hand in hand, step by step, week by week. You are doing holy, beautiful work.

COUPLES ACTIVITY: HALFWAY CELEBRATION

1. Celebrate the Journey

Take time this week to sit together and reflect:

- What has been the most meaningful part of this devotional journey so far?
- What has been hard or surprising?
- Where have we seen even small shifts in our love, trust, or faith?

2. Speak Blessing Over Each Other

Take turns looking into each other's eyes and saying: *"Thank you for walking this journey with me. I bless you to keep growing, keep loving, and keep becoming all God made you to be. I'm proud of you. I love you."*

3. Do Something Fun Together

Mark the halfway point with something light and joyful—a simple date, a walk, a favorite meal, or just dancing in the kitchen. Let celebration be part of your spiritual life!

FINAL ENCOURAGEMENT

You are halfway through—and God's not done with you yet.

The best is still ahead.
The breakthroughs are still coming.
The deep waters of love, grace, and intimacy are still waiting to be explored.

Keep going.
Keep loving.
Keep holding onto each other and onto Him.

I am cheering you on—and so is heaven.

WEEK 27
GRATITUDE—SEEING AND NAMING THE GOOD

MEDITATION SCRIPTURES

"Give thanks to the Lord, for He is good; His love endures forever."—Psalm 136:1 (NIV)

"In everything give thanks; for this is the will of God in Christ Jesus for you."—1 Thessalonians 5:18 (NKJV)

"Every good gift and every perfect gift is from above, and comes down from the Father of lights."—James 1:17 (NKJV)

GUIDED MEDITATION ON SCRIPTURE

Sit quietly together. Take a few slow breaths, letting your mind settle.

Read the scriptures aloud, slowly, pausing after each: give thanks… in everything… every good gift.

Reflect silently:

ی What gifts has God placed in our marriage that we've stopped noticing?

ٮ What qualities or actions in my spouse am I grateful for, but rarely name out loud?

ٮ Where is God inviting us to trade complaint or weariness for gratitude and wonder?

Sit in stillness, letting gratefulness rise gently in your heart.

QUOTE FOR TODAY

"In all created things discern the providence and wisdom of God, and in all things give Him thanks."

—*Teresa of Ávila*

WORD FOR THE WEEK

Gratitude is a holy practice—and one of the most powerful ways to nourish a marriage. It shifts your focus from what's missing to what's present, from irritation to appreciation, from scarcity to abundance. Gratitude doesn't mean ignoring hard things; it means intentionally seeing the good, even in small and ordinary moments.

In marriage, it's easy to drift into taking each other for granted. We stop noticing the kindness, the small helps, the enduring love that carries us daily. Or we start focusing on what our spouse isn't doing, forgetting the many things they are offering. Gratitude softens the heart, opens the eyes, and renews affection.

God's Word invites us to give thanks in everything—not necessarily for everything, but in every situation, we can find something to lift in praise: a lesson learned, a moment shared, a grace received, a strength discovered. Gratitude draws us closer to God, and it draws us closer to each other.

This week, make gratitude your practice. Name the good. Celebrate the small. Speak thanks often. Watch how it warms the atmosphere of your home and tenderizes your love.

PSALM TO MEDITATE ON

"Bless the Lord, O my soul, and forget not all His benefits."— Psalm 103:2 (NKJV)

GUIDED MEDITATION ON THE PSALM

Read Psalm 103:2 aloud slowly.

Ask together:

- ی Lord, what blessings have we forgotten or overlooked?
- ی How can we practice gratefulness toward You and toward each other this week?

Picture your hearts opening wide, like hands lifted in thanksgiving.

DECLARATIONS FOR THE WEEK

We declare:

- ی We are grateful for God's goodness and presence in our marriage.

- ٮ We choose to notice and name the blessings we've been given.
- ٮ We thank God for each other—as gifts, not entitlements.
- ٮ Gratitude fills our home, softens our hearts, and renews our love.
- ٮ We are a thankful, joyful, grace-filled couple.

COMMUNION PRAYER

(Prepare bread (or a cracker) and a small cup of juice. Together, hold the bread and pray).

Lord Jesus Christ, we come before You now, humbled and grateful. You are the Bread of Life, the true Manna from heaven. You gave Your body to be broken for us, that we might be made whole—spirit, soul, and body. You poured out Your blood as the cup of the new covenant, that we might be cleansed, forgiven, and reconciled to God.

We pause to remember Your sacrifice. We remember Your wounds, Your love, Your victory. We remember that You carried our sickness, our grief, our sins, and our shame upon Yourself at the cross (see Isaiah 53:4–5). You conquered death, hell, and the grave, and You rose again, so that we might share in Your life.

We confess, Lord, that we need You. We bring before You every place in our lives and marriage where we are weak, divided, hurting, or burdened. We ask for Your forgiveness for where we have spoken in anger, withheld love, carried resentment, or failed to honor one another. Wash us clean, Jesus—in Your mercy, cover us with Your righteousness.

As we eat this bread, we receive Your healing. Heal our hearts where they are wounded. Heal our minds where they are anxious or tormented. Heal our bodies where they are sick or weak. Heal our marriage where it has been strained or broken. Let the same power that raised You from the dead now flow through us. Jesus, You are the greatest gift—the treasure of our hearts, the joy of our souls, the anchor of our marriage. Thank You for all You have done, all You are doing, and all You will do. As we eat this bread, we remember Your body—given in love.

(Eat the bread)

As we drink this cup, we renew our covenant with You and with each other. We declare that we are Yours, and You are ours. We belong to You—as individuals and as a couple. Strengthen the bond between us. Let our love be patient, kind, humble, and enduring. Let forgiveness flow freely in our home. Let Your peace reign over our household. Jesus, thank You for Your blood, poured out for forgiveness and new life. As we drink this cup, we receive Your blood—poured out in grace.

(Drink the cup)

Jesus, fill us with Your Spirit. Unite us in Your love. Draw us deeper into the mystery of union with You—that we may be one as You and the Father are one. Teach us to love one another with Your supernatural love. Teach us to walk in Your ways. Teach us to see our marriage not only as partnership, but as a holy vessel that carries Your glory into this world.

We receive now—with faith and joy—the blessings You have promised. Blessings of peace, healing, provision, restoration, protection, wisdom, and overflowing grace. We stand in agreement, as one, declaring that no weapon formed against us shall prosper. We break every assignment of the enemy against our lives and marriage. We release blessing over our future, over our family, and over the generations to come.

We thank You for each other. We thank You for every small and large blessing in our lives. Teach us to be grateful people, not just with our words, but with our posture of heart.

Thank You, Jesus. Amen.

FINAL WORD

Gratitude is the secret soil where love grows. Water your marriage this week with thankfulness—spoken, written, and shown—and watch how joy begins to bloom again.

COUPLES ACTIVITY: "GRATITUDE EXCHANGE"

Set aside 20 minutes this week to sit together and name 3 things you're grateful for in each other.

You can start small or big:

- A simple daily habit they do that helps.
- A character quality you admire.
- A moment they supported or loved you well.

After sharing, pray together: *"Lord, thank You for these gifts. Help us keep noticing and cherishing them."*

WEEK 28
FORGIVENESS—LIVING FREE, LOVING DEEPLY

MEDITATION SCRIPTURES

"Be kind to one another, tenderhearted, forgiving one another, as God in Christ forgave you."—Ephesians 4:32 (ESV)

"For if you forgive other people when they sin against you, your heavenly Father will also forgive you."—Matthew 6:14 (NIV)

"Above all, love each other deeply, because love covers over a multitude of sins."—1 Peter 4:8 (NIV)

GUIDED MEDITATION ON SCRIPTURE

Sit quietly together, take a few slow breaths.

Read the scriptures aloud, slowly, letting the words *tenderhearted… forgiving… love covers…* wash over your minds and hearts.

Reflect silently:

- Are there small (or large) offenses we've been holding onto?
- Where do we need to extend or ask for forgiveness?

- What would it feel like to lay those burdens down and choose freedom?

Invite God to soften and heal places where pain or resentment may have settled.

QUOTE FOR TODAY

"All bitterness is forgiven the moment we realize that the heart we are angry at is just as wounded as our own."

—Thomas Merton

WORD FOR THE WEEK

Forgiveness is the oil that keeps marriage from breaking under the weight of human imperfection. Without it, small hurts turn into walls, disappointments become resentments, and old wounds keep shaping new interactions. But with forgiveness, love stays tender, open, and resilient.

Forgiveness doesn't mean pretending nothing happened or excusing wrong. It means releasing the right to punish, choosing mercy over vengeance, and letting God be the healer of what's broken. Sometimes forgiveness is offered in a moment; other times, it's a process repeated over and over.

In marriage, both giving and asking for forgiveness are vital. Saying "I was wrong" or "I forgive you" creates space for intimacy to grow again. It takes courage and humility but it leads to deep freedom, not only for the person forgiven but for the one forgiving.

This week, let forgiveness be your practice. Don't wait for perfect apologies or ideal circumstances. Offer grace as freely as you yourself have received it from Christ. In doing so, you mirror His heart and you keep your love strong.

PSALM TO MEDITATE ON

"As far as the east is from the west, so far has He removed our transgressions from us."—Psalm 103:12 (NKJV)

GUIDED MEDITATION ON THE PSALM

Read Psalm 103:12 slowly, almost as a whisper.

Ask together:

- ك Lord, where do we need to forgive?
- ك Where do we need to receive forgiveness—from You, from each other, from ourselves?

Picture God lifting the weight of offenses and casting them away, leaving your hearts light and free.

DECLARATIONS FOR THE WEEK

We declare:

- ك Our marriage is a place of grace, not grudges.
- ك We forgive quickly, fully, and freely, just as God forgives us.
- ك We are not held captive by past mistakes.

- ى We walk in humility, tenderness, and love.
- ى Our love is deep, strong, and renewed through forgiveness.

COMMUNION PRAYER

(Prepare bread (or a cracker) and a small cup of juice. Together, hold the bread and pray).

Lord Jesus Christ, we come before You now, humbled and grateful. You are the Bread of Life, the true Manna from heaven. You gave Your body to be broken for us, that we might be made whole—spirit, soul, and body. You poured out Your blood as the cup of the new covenant, that we might be cleansed, forgiven, and reconciled to God.

We pause to remember Your sacrifice. We remember Your wounds, Your love, Your victory. We remember that You carried our sickness, our grief, our sins, and our shame upon Yourself at the cross (see Isaiah 53:4–5). You conquered death, hell, and the grave, and You rose again, so that we might share in Your life.

We confess, Lord, that we need You. We bring before You every place in our lives and marriage where we are weak, divided, hurting, or burdened. We ask for Your forgiveness for where we have spoken in anger, withheld love, carried resentment, or failed to honor one another. Wash us clean, Jesus—in Your mercy, cover us with Your righteousness.

As we eat this bread, we receive Your healing. Heal our hearts where they are wounded. Heal our minds where they are anxious or tormented. Heal our bodies where they are sick or weak. Heal our

213

marriage where it has been strained or broken. Let the same power that raised You from the dead now flow through us. Jesus, You bore our sins, carried our sorrows, and forgave us fully at the cross. Thank You for setting us free. As we eat this bread, we remember Your body—broken so we could be healed.

(Eat the bread)

As we drink this cup, we renew our covenant with You and with each other. We declare that we are Yours, and You are ours. We belong to You—as individuals and as a couple. Strengthen the bond between us. Let our love be patient, kind, humble, and enduring. Let forgiveness flow freely in our home. Let Your peace reign over our household. Jesus, thank You for Your blood, poured out for forgiveness and new life. As we drink this cup, we receive Your blood—poured out so we could be forgiven.

(Drink the cup)

Jesus, fill us with Your Spirit. Unite us in Your love. Draw us deeper into the mystery of union with You—that we may be one as You and the Father are one. Teach us to love one another with Your supernatural love. Teach us to walk in Your ways. Teach us to see our marriage not only as partnership, but as a holy vessel that carries Your glory into this world.

We receive now—with faith and joy—the blessings You have promised. Blessings of peace, healing, provision, restoration, protection, wisdom, and overflowing grace. We stand in agreement, as one, declaring that no weapon formed against us shall prosper. We break every assignment of the enemy against our lives and marriage. We release blessing over our future, over our family, and over the generations to come.

We release any offenses we've held onto. We forgive each other. We forgive ourselves. We receive Your mercy, and we choose to walk in love.

Thank You, Jesus. Amen.

FINAL WORD

Forgiveness doesn't weaken love—it strengthens it. Let this week be a time of softening, surrender, and starting fresh. You are not defined by past wounds; you are shaped by present grace.

COUPLES ACTIVITY: "THE FORGIVENESS EXCHANGE"

Set aside a quiet, gentle moment this week to each share:

- و One area where you need forgiveness.
- و One way you want to offer forgiveness.

After sharing, say to each other: *"I forgive you, and I love you."*

End with a simple prayer: *"Lord, help us forgive as You forgive, and love as You love."*

WEEK 29
RESTORATION—GOD MAKES ALL THINGS NEW

MEDITATION SCRIPTURES

"And the God of all grace… after you have suffered a little while, will Himself restore you and make you strong, firm, and steadfast."—1 Peter 5:10 (NIV)

"Behold, I am making all things new."—Revelation 21:5 (NKJV)

"He restores my soul; He leads me in the paths of righteousness for His name's sake."—Psalm 23:3 (NKJV)

GUIDED MEDITATION ON SCRIPTURE

Sit together quietly, maybe with hands joined or simply close.

Read the scriptures aloud slowly, letting the words *restore… make all things new… He restores my soul* wash over you.

Reflect silently:

- ى What areas of our marriage feel worn, wounded, or dry?
- ى Where do we long to see God's restoration—in our trust, friendship, intimacy, laughter, or faith?

ﺱ How might we open space for His restoring work?

Rest in quiet, inviting God to breathe new life into you both.

QUOTE FOR TODAY

"God is a God of new beginnings. Nothing is so ruined that His love cannot rebuild it."

—*Thomas à Kempis*

WORD FOR THE WEEK

Every marriage goes through seasons of weariness, disappointment, or fracture. Even in strong relationships, small cracks can form: miscommunications, unmet needs, loss of tenderness, or simply the grind of life. But we serve a God who specializes in restoration—not just fixing what's broken, but making it new, often stronger and more beautiful than before.

Restoration begins with honesty: naming what has been hurt, what has been lost, or what has been neglected. It continues with humility: opening space for forgiveness, for rebuilding, for learning new ways of loving. And it thrives through hope—believing that no matter how dry the ground, God can send rain.

Restoration doesn't erase the past, but it redeems it. The same hands that bear the scars of crucifixion are the hands that make all things new. In your marriage, He longs to restore your joy, your unity, your intimacy, your sense of purpose together.

This week, invite God's restoring presence into your marriage. Speak it over each other. Pray it into the weary places. Choose one small way to refresh love. Let the God of grace renew you.

PSALM TO MEDITATE ON

"Those who sow in tears shall reap in joy. He who continually goes forth weeping, bearing seed for sowing, shall doubtless come again with rejoicing, bringing his sheaves with him."—Psalm 126:5–6 (NKJV)

GUIDED MEDITATION ON THE PSALM

Read Psalm 126:5-6 slowly.

Ask together:

- Lord, what tears or struggles are You turning into joy?
- Where do we need to keep sowing hope, even before we see the harvest?

Picture God planting seeds of restoration in your hearts and promising a future harvest of joy.

DECLARATIONS FOR THE WEEK

We declare:

- God is restoring our hearts, our marriage, and our home.
- What has been broken, He is making whole.
- What has been dry, He is watering with new life.

- ﺱ We are not stuck in the past; we are stepping into new beginnings.
- ﺱ Our marriage reflects the redeeming love of God.

COMMUNION PRAYER

(Prepare bread (or a cracker) and a small cup of juice. Together, hold the bread and pray).

Lord Jesus Christ, we come before You now, humbled and grateful. You are the Bread of Life, the true Manna from heaven. You gave Your body to be broken for us, that we might be made whole—spirit, soul, and body. You poured out Your blood as the cup of the new covenant, that we might be cleansed, forgiven, and reconciled to God.

We pause to remember Your sacrifice. We remember Your wounds, Your love, Your victory. We remember that You carried our sickness, our grief, our sins, and our shame upon Yourself at the cross (see Isaiah 53:4–5). You conquered death, hell, and the grave, and You rose again, so that we might share in Your life.

We confess, Lord, that we need You. We bring before You every place in our lives and marriage where we are weak, divided, hurting, or burdened. We ask for Your forgiveness for where we have spoken in anger, withheld love, carried resentment, or failed to honor one another. Wash us clean, Jesus—in Your mercy, cover us with Your righteousness.

As we eat this bread, we receive Your healing. Heal our hearts where they are wounded. Heal our minds where they are anxious or

tormented. Heal our bodies where they are sick or weak. Heal our marriage where it has been strained or broken. Let the same power that raised You from the dead now flow through us. Jesus, You are the Restorer of our souls. You bring dead things to life, dry bones to dancing, empty places to overflowing. As we eat this bread, we remember Your body—broken to heal and restore us.

(Eat the bread)

As we drink this cup, we renew our covenant with You and with each other. We declare that we are Yours, and You are ours. We belong to You—as individuals and as a couple. Strengthen the bond between us. Let our love be patient, kind, humble, and enduring. Let forgiveness flow freely in our home. Let Your peace reign over our household. Jesus, thank You for Your blood, poured out for forgiveness and new life. As we drink this cup, we receive Your blood—poured out to make all things new.

(Drink the cup)

Jesus, fill us with Your Spirit. Unite us in Your love. Draw us deeper into the mystery of union with You—that we may be one as You and the Father are one. Teach us to love one another with Your supernatural love. Teach us to walk in Your ways. Teach us to see our marriage not only as partnership, but as a holy vessel that carries Your glory into this world.

We receive now—with faith and joy—the blessings You have promised. Blessings of peace, healing, provision, restoration, protection, wisdom, and overflowing grace. We stand in agreement, as one, declaring that no weapon formed against us shall prosper. We break every assignment of the enemy against our lives and marriage. We release blessing over our future, over our family, and over the generations to come.

We bring You the places in our marriage that need Your touch. Restore us, Lord. Renew our love, our trust, our laughter, and our purpose. Make us strong, firm, and steadfast in You.

Thank You, Jesus. Amen.

FINAL WORD

Restoration is not just God's work—it's His joy. Trust Him to rebuild what's been lost, to refresh what's grown tired, and to make your marriage new in ways you cannot yet imagine.

COUPLES ACTIVITY: "THE RESTORATION CONVERSATION"

Set aside time this week to gently ask each other:

- ى Where do you feel most weary or stretched in our marriage?
- ى What is one area you long to see refreshed or healed?
- ى How can we, together, invite God's restoring work?

Pray together, laying these areas before God. Then, choose one small action you can take to nurture restoration—maybe a date, a deeper conversation, or a simple act of care.

WEEK 30
SERVING EACH OTHER—LOVE MADE VISIBLE

MEDITATION SCRIPTURES

"For even the Son of Man did not come to be served, but to serve, and to give His life as a ransom for many."—Mark 10:45 (NIV)

"Through love serve one another."—Galatians 5:13 (NKJV)

"Now that I, your Lord and Teacher, have washed your feet, you also should wash one another's feet."—John 13:14 (NIV)

GUIDED MEDITATION ON SCRIPTURE

Sit quietly together. Breathe deeply, slowly.

Read the scriptures aloud, slowly. Let the words *serve... wash one another's feet... through love* settle into your heart.

Reflect silently:

- How have we been serving each other well lately?
- Where have we been waiting to be served instead of serve?
- What small acts of love could we offer this week to lighten each other's load?

Rest in God's presence, asking Him to give you a servant's heart.

QUOTE FOR TODAY

"The measure of love is to love without measure."
—*St. Francis of Assisi*

WORD FOR THE WEEK

Love is not just a feeling—it is a practice, and one of its most beautiful expressions is service. When we serve each other, we make love visible: in the meal cooked, the chore done without being asked, the listening ear, the cup of tea, the gentle word, the quiet prayer.

Jesus modelled this kind of love when He knelt to wash His disciples' feet—an act of humility, tenderness, and care. In marriage, we are invited to do the same: not waiting until the other "deserves" it, but freely offering ourselves in small, daily ways. This builds trust, deepens affection, and strengthens the bond of oneness.

Sometimes we resist serving because we feel tired, unnoticed, or resentful. But when we remember that love is a gift we offer, not a transaction we measure, serving becomes a joy, not a burden. And often, as we give, we find our own hearts refreshed.

This week, make it your goal to serve each other with gladness. Find one small way each day to say, *"I see you. I love you. I am here for you."* Watch how God meets you in the ordinary, transforming it into something holy.

PSALM TO MEDITATE ON

"Serve the Lord with gladness; come before His presence with singing."—Psalm 100:2 (NKJV)

GUIDED MEDITATION ON THE PSALM

Read Psalm 100:2 aloud slowly.

Ask together:

- ﮑ Lord, how can we serve You by serving each other?
- ﮑ What small act of love do You want to inspire in us this week?

Picture your service as a fragrant offering rising up to God, bringing Him joy.

DECLARATIONS FOR THE WEEK

We declare:

- ﮑ We serve each other gladly, as an act of love.
- ﮑ Our small acts of care are sacred in God's eyes.
- ﮑ We give, not to earn, but to bless.
- ﮑ Serving draws us closer to each other and to Christ.
- ﮑ Our home is filled with humility, kindness, and generosity.

COMMUNION PRAYER

(Prepare bread (or a cracker) and a small cup of juice. Together, hold the bread and pray).

Lord Jesus Christ, we come before You now, humbled and grateful. You are the Bread of Life, the true Manna from heaven. You gave Your body to be broken for us, that we might be made whole—spirit, soul, and body. You poured out Your blood as the cup of the new covenant, that we might be cleansed, forgiven, and reconciled to God.

We pause to remember Your sacrifice. We remember Your wounds, Your love, Your victory. We remember that You carried our sickness, our grief, our sins, and our shame upon Yourself at the cross (see Isaiah 53:4–5). You conquered death, hell, and the grave, and You rose again, so that we might share in Your life.

We confess, Lord, that we need You. We bring before You every place in our lives and marriage where we are weak, divided, hurting, or burdened. We ask for Your forgiveness for where we have spoken in anger, withheld love, carried resentment, or failed to honor one another. Wash us clean, Jesus—in Your mercy, cover us with Your righteousness.

As we eat this bread, we receive Your healing. Heal our hearts where they are wounded. Heal our minds where they are anxious or tormented. Heal our bodies where they are sick or weak. Heal our marriage where it has been strained or broken. Let the same power that raised You from the dead now flow through us. Jesus, You stooped low to serve, to wash, to heal, to love. You gave Your life freely, so we might live. As we eat this bread, we remember Your body—given in service for us.

(Eat the bread)

As we drink this cup, we renew our covenant with You and with each other. We declare that we are Yours, and You are ours. We belong to You—as individuals and as a couple. Strengthen the bond between us. Let our love be patient, kind, humble, and enduring. Let forgiveness flow freely in our home. Let Your peace reign over our household. Jesus, thank You for Your blood, poured out for forgiveness and new life. As we drink this cup, we receive Your blood—poured out in love.

(Drink the cup)

Jesus, fill us with Your Spirit. Unite us in Your love. Draw us deeper into the mystery of union with You—that we may be one as You and the Father are one. Teach us to love one another with Your supernatural love. Teach us to walk in Your ways. Teach us to see our marriage not only as partnership, but as a holy vessel that carries Your glory into this world.

We receive now—with faith and joy—the blessings You have promised. Blessings of peace, healing, provision, restoration, protection, wisdom, and overflowing grace. We stand in agreement, as one, declaring that no weapon formed against us shall prosper. We break every assignment of the enemy against our lives and marriage.

We release blessing over our future, over our family, and over the generations to come.

Help us, Lord, to serve one another with joy, to carry each other's burdens, to offer love in small, daily ways. Make our marriage a reflection of Your self-giving heart.

Thank You, Jesus. Amen.

COUPLES ACTIVITY: "SECRET SERVICE CHALLENGE"

Each of you secretly choose one daily act of service for the other this week—something small but meaningful.

Examples:

- Make their morning coffee or breakfast.
- Do a chore they dislike.
- Write a short encouraging note.
- Offer a back rub or foot massage.
- Pray for them quietly.

At the end of the week, come together and share what you noticed, how it felt, and thank each other.

COUPLES ACTIVITY

THE GIFT OF SMALL ACTS

This activity is called "The Gift of Small Acts" because sometimes the smallest actions carry the deepest love.

STEP 1: NAME ONE NEED

Sit together for 10–15 minutes this week. Each of you gently share: *"One small way you feel loved when I help or support you."*

Examples: *"When you help tidy up the kitchen," "When you check in on how my day was," "When you pray out loud for me," "When you bring me a cup of tea," "When you hug me at the end of the day."*

Important: Focus on something doable and specific, not vague or overwhelming.

STEP 2: COMMIT TO SHOW UP

For the next 3–5 days, each of you commit to doing that one small act of service for the other. It's okay if it's imperfect. The point is intentionality, not performance.

STEP 3: CELEBRATE

At the end of the week, take 15 minutes to sit down and reflect:

- What did it feel like to give? To receive?
- Did anything shift in your mood, connection, or atmosphere at home?
- How can we keep small acts of love part of our everyday rhythm?
- End by praying together or simply saying: *"Thank you for loving me in this way."*

MOTIVATION AND ENCOURAGEMENT: WHY SMALL SERVICE MATTERS

Sometimes we think love has to be big and dramatic—grand dates, expensive gifts, big words. But in God's eyes, love is often most visible in the quiet, humble, daily acts that say, *"I see you. I'm with you. I'm for you."*

When Jesus washed His disciples' feet, He showed that love isn't measured by status or scorekeeping but by sacrifice, humility, and kindness.

In marriage, every time you serve each other—whether it's making coffee, folding laundry, listening well, or offering a hug—you are mirroring the heart of Christ.

Here's the beautiful truth: when you serve in love, both hearts are blessed. The one who serves is filled with joy. The one who receives feels seen and cherished. And God smiles over both.

So this week, don't underestimate the power of small things. In God's hands, they are sacred, healing, and strong enough to shape a lifetime.

EXPANSION

(service, hospitality, laughter, transitions, courage)

WEEK 31
WALKING IN UNITY—SHARING VISION, SHARING PURPOSE

MEDITATION SCRIPTURES

"Can two walk together, unless they are agreed?"—Amos 3:3 (NKJV)

"Make every effort to keep the unity of the Spirit through the bond of peace."—Ephesians 4:3 (NIV)

"I in them, and You in Me—so that they may be brought to complete unity. Then the world will know that You sent Me and have loved them even as You have loved Me."—John 17:23 (NIV)

GUIDED MEDITATION ON SCRIPTURE

Sit quietly together, hands joined if you like.

Read the scriptures aloud slowly. Let the words *walk together… unity… bond of peace… complete unity* soak in.

Reflect silently:

> ی Where are we walking well in unity—emotionally, spiritually, practically?

ى Where are we struggling to stay aligned or understand each other?

ى What shared purpose has God placed on our marriage?

Invite the Holy Spirit to show you not just how to "get along," but how to walk together in deeper unity and shared calling.

QUOTE FOR TODAY

"Love unites, and in that union, the many become one in God."
—*Meister Eckhart*

WORD FOR THE WEEK

Unity in marriage is not the same as sameness. You are two unique people, with different perspectives, gifts, and personalities. But unity is about walking in the same direction—committed to shared love, shared faith, and shared purpose.

When couples lack unity, even small decisions can feel like battles, and dreams can pull them apart. But when couples cultivate unity, they become a powerful team—supporting each other's callings, building together, lifting each other higher, and reflecting God's heart to the world.

Unity takes intentional work: listening deeply, making space for both voices, setting common goals, and inviting God to reveal His dreams for you as a couple. It also takes humility: laying down personal agendas when needed, choosing peace over pride, and remembering you are on the same side.

This week, ask God to refresh your shared vision. What has He put on your hearts to build, nurture, protect, or bring into the world— together? Whether it's raising a family, serving your community, creating beauty, building a business, or simply being a home of peace, He has a purpose for you as one.

PSALM TO MEDITATE ON

"How good and pleasant it is when God's people live together in unity! For there the Lord bestows His blessing, even life forevermore."—Psalm 133:1, 3 (NIV)

GUIDED MEDITATION ON THE PSALM

Read Psalm 133:1-3 aloud slowly.

Ask together:

- Lord, where are You calling us into deeper unity?
- What shared dreams or purposes do You want to rekindle in us?

Picture God pouring fresh oil of blessing over your marriage, refreshing your love and purpose.

DECLARATIONS FOR THE WEEK

We declare:

- We walk in unity, love, and peace.
- We are united in purpose, guided by God's hand.

- We listen, respect, and honor one another's voice.
- We are stronger together than apart.

Our marriage is a testimony of God's unifying love.

COMMUNION PRAYER

(Prepare bread (or a cracker) and a small cup of juice. Together, hold the bread and pray).

Lord Jesus Christ, we come before You now, humbled and grateful. You are the Bread of Life, the true Manna from heaven. You gave Your body to be broken for us, that we might be made whole—spirit, soul, and body. You poured out Your blood as the cup of the new covenant, that we might be cleansed, forgiven, and reconciled to God.

We pause to remember Your sacrifice. We remember Your wounds, Your love, Your victory. We remember that You carried our sickness, our grief, our sins, and our shame upon Yourself at the cross (see Isaiah 53:4–5). You conquered death, hell, and the grave, and You rose again, so that we might share in Your life.

We confess, Lord, that we need You. We bring before You every place in our lives and marriage where we are weak, divided, hurting, or burdened. We ask for Your forgiveness for where we have spoken in anger, withheld love, carried resentment, or failed to honor one another. Wash us clean, Jesus—in Your mercy, cover us with Your righteousness.

As we eat this bread, we receive Your healing. Heal our hearts where they are wounded. Heal our minds where they are anxious or tormented. Heal our bodies where they are sick or weak. Heal our marriage where it has been strained or broken. Let the same power that raised You from the dead now flow through us. Jesus, You prayed that we would be one—just as You and the Father are one. You joined our hearts not just in love, but in shared calling. As we eat this bread, we remember Your body, uniting us to Yourself and to each other.

(Eat the bread)

As we drink this cup, we renew our covenant with You and with each other. We declare that we are Yours, and You are ours. We belong to You—as individuals and as a couple. Strengthen the bond between us. Let our love be patient, kind, humble, and enduring. Let forgiveness flow freely in our home. Let Your peace reign over our household. Jesus, thank You for Your blood, poured out for forgiveness and new life. As we drink this cup, we receive Your blood, binding us in covenant love.

(Drink the cup)

Jesus, fill us with Your Spirit. Unite us in Your love. Draw us deeper into the mystery of union with You—that we may be one as You and the Father are one. Teach us to love one another with Your supernatural love. Teach us to walk in Your ways. Teach us to see our marriage not only as partnership, but as a holy vessel that carries Your glory into this world.

We receive now—with faith and joy—the blessings You have promised. Blessings of peace, healing, provision, restoration, protection, wisdom, and overflowing grace. We stand in agreement, as one, declaring that no weapon formed against us shall prosper. We break every assignment of the enemy against our lives and marriage. We release blessing over our future, over our family, and over the generations to come.

We surrender our separate plans. We say yes to Your shared purpose for us. Make us one in spirit, one in love, and one in mission.

Thank You, Jesus. Amen.

FINAL WORD

Unity is not found by accident; it is built with intention. This week, slow down, listen well, dream together, and ask God to show you why He joined your lives—not just for each other, but for His purposes.

COUPLES ACTIVITY: "OUR SHARED PURPOSE CONVERSATION"

Set aside time this week to ask each other:

- ﺱ What do you feel God has put on your heart in this season?
- ﺱ What dreams or purposes do we share?
- ﺱ How can we support each other's callings and grow as a team?

After sharing, pray together: *"Lord, align our hearts with Your purpose. Make us a united couple, a light for Your glory."*

WEEK 32
PRAYING TOGETHER—STRENGTHENING THE BOND OF THREE

MEDITATION SCRIPTURES

"Again I say to you, that if two of you agree on earth concerning anything that they ask, it will be done for them by My Father in heaven. For where two or three are gathered together in My name, I am there in the midst of them."—Matthew 18:19–20 (NKJV)

"They all joined together constantly in prayer."—Acts 1:14 (NIV)

"Devote yourselves to prayer, being watchful and thankful."—Colossians 4:2 (NIV)

GUIDED MEDITATION ON SCRIPTURE

Sit quietly together, maybe holding hands or sitting in comfortable stillness.

Read the scriptures aloud slowly. Let the words *agree… gathered in My name… joined constantly… devote yourselves* settle into your hearts.

Reflect silently:

- How has prayer shaped our marriage so far?
- What holds us back from praying more often or more deeply together?
- How might God be inviting us to strengthen our bond through prayer this season?

Pause together, inviting the Holy Spirit to stir fresh desire for shared prayer.

QUOTE FOR TODAY

"Prayer unites the soul to God. But when two pray as one, it is as though they lift the whole world together into His hands."
—Julian of Norwich

WORD FOR THE WEEK

Praying together is one of the simplest yet most powerful ways to deepen intimacy, heal hurts, and invite God's presence into your marriage. And yet for many couples, it's one of the hardest habits to build. Life feels busy, prayer feels awkward, or past disappointments make it hard to trust God together.

But Scripture shows us that when two agree, when two gather, when two lift their voices together, something shifts, not only in heaven but in the hearts of those who pray. Prayer isn't about perfect words or polished faith; it's about showing up together before God, in weakness and hope, in need and gratitude, and saying, *Here we are, Lord. We need You.*

Couples who pray together become stronger, softer, and more united. Prayer softens resentment, builds compassion, and aligns you with God's purposes. It reminds you that you are not just a couple—you are a cord of three strands (see Ecclesiastes 4:12), with Christ at the center.

This week, take small, gentle steps to pray together. It could be a whispered prayer before bed, a blessing over meals, or a few minutes holding hands and lifting your concerns. Keep it simple. Keep it real. And trust God to meet you there.

PSALM TO MEDITATE ON

"The Lord is near to all who call on Him, to all who call on Him in truth."—Psalm 145:18 (NIV)

GUIDED MEDITATION ON THE PSALM

Read Psalm 145:18 aloud slowly.

Ask together:

- Lord, where do we need to invite You more intentionally into our marriage through prayer?
- What burdens, joys, or dreams do You want us to bring to You together?

Picture God drawing near as you call on Him, His presence gentle and faithful.

DECLARATIONS FOR THE WEEK

We declare:

- ى Our marriage is a house of prayer.
- ى We are not alone; God is with us in every need and joy.
- ى We lift each other, our family, and our future to God daily.
- ى Prayer softens our hearts and strengthens our bond.
- ى We walk in unity, hope, and love, anchored in Christ.

COMMUNION PRAYER

(Prepare bread (or a cracker) and a small cup of juice. Together, hold the bread and pray).

Lord Jesus Christ, we come before You now, humbled and grateful. You are the Bread of Life, the true Manna from heaven. You gave Your body to be broken for us, that we might be made whole—spirit, soul, and body. You poured out Your blood as the cup of the new covenant, that we might be cleansed, forgiven, and reconciled to God.

We pause to remember Your sacrifice. We remember Your wounds, Your love, Your victory. We remember that You carried our sickness, our grief, our sins, and our shame upon Yourself at the cross (see Isaiah 53:4–5). You conquered death, hell, and the grave, and You rose again, so that we might share in Your life.

We confess, Lord, that we need You. We bring before You every place in our lives and marriage where we are weak, divided, hurting, or burdened. We ask for Your forgiveness for where we have spoken in anger, withheld love, carried resentment, or failed to honor one another. Wash us clean, Jesus—in Your mercy, cover us with Your righteousness.

As we eat this bread, we receive Your healing. Heal our hearts where they are wounded. Heal our minds where they are anxious or tormented. Heal our bodies where they are sick or weak. Heal our marriage where it has been strained or broken. Let the same power that raised You from the dead now flow through us. Jesus, You are our intercessor, our mediator, and our closest friend. Thank You for always praying for us and inviting us to pray with You. As we eat this bread, we remember Your body, opening the way to the Father.

(Eat the bread)

As we drink this cup, we renew our covenant with You and with each other. We declare that we are Yours, and You are ours. We belong to You—as individuals and as a couple. Strengthen the bond between us. Let our love be patient, kind, humble, and enduring. Let forgiveness flow freely in our home. Let Your peace reign over our household. Jesus, thank You for Your blood, poured out for forgiveness and new life. As we drink this cup, we receive Your blood, making us one with You and with each other.

(Drink the cup)

Jesus, fill us with Your Spirit. Unite us in Your love. Draw us deeper into the mystery of union with You—that we may be one as You and the Father are one. Teach us to love one another with Your supernatural love. Teach us to walk in Your ways. Teach us to see our marriage not only as partnership, but as a holy vessel that carries Your glory into this world.

We receive now—with faith and joy—the blessings You have promised. Blessings of peace, healing, provision, restoration, protection, wisdom, and overflowing grace. We stand in agreement, as one, declaring that no weapon formed against us shall prosper. We break every assignment of the enemy against our lives and marriage. We release blessing over our future, over our family, and over the generations to come.

Teach us to pray together, Lord—not out of duty, but out of love. Let our prayers be simple, true, and full of trust. Let them bind us closer to You and to each other.

Thank You, Jesus. Amen.

FINAL WORD

Praying together is not about getting it "right"—it's about showing up, together, before the God who loves you. This week, let shared prayer be the quiet, steady rhythm that strengthens your love.

COUPLES ACTIVITY: "ONE-MINUTE PRAYER HABIT"

Commit this week to pray together once a day—even just for one minute.

It could be:

- A simple thank-you prayer before sleep.
- A short blessing over each other's day.
- Holding hands and lifting one specific need or joy.

At the end of the week, share: *"How did this feel? What did we notice in our hearts and home?"*

WEEK 33
TRUSTING GOD WITH OUR FUTURE— LETTING GO, MOVING FORWARD TOGETHER

MEDITATION SCRIPTURES

"For I know the plans I have for you," says the Lord, "plans to prosper you and not to harm you, plans to give you hope and a future."—Jeremiah 29:11 (NIV)

"Trust in the Lord with all your heart, and lean not on your own understanding; in all your ways submit to Him, and He will make your paths straight."—Proverbs 3:5–6 (NIV)

"Commit your way to the Lord; trust also in Him, and He shall bring it to pass."—Psalm 37:5 (NKJV)

GUIDED MEDITATION ON SCRIPTURE

Sit together quietly, maybe holding hands or resting close.

Read the scriptures aloud slowly. Let the words *plans... trust... submit... commit... hope and a future* rest in your hearts.

Reflect silently:

- ﻼ Where are we anxious or uncertain about our future as a couple—finances, health, family, work, purpose?
- ﻼ What dreams or fears have we not yet brought fully before God?
- ﻼ What would it look like to surrender our future to Him in trust and hope?

Breathe slowly, picturing yourselves placing your future into God's faithful hands.

QUOTE FOR TODAY

"God's plans are greater than our imagining, more loving than our asking, and more perfect than our planning."
—*St. Teresa of Avila*

WORD FOR THE WEEK

Every couple carries questions about the future: *Will we be okay? What is God calling us to? How do we handle the uncertainties ahead?* It's easy to become anxious or controlling, to lean on our own plans, or to fear what we cannot see. But God invites us to a different posture—one of trust, surrender, and hope.

Trusting God with your future doesn't mean passivity or ignoring practical planning. It means anchoring all you do in the confidence that God is good, wise, and present. It means making plans but holding them lightly. It means dreaming but inviting God to reshape those dreams. It means walking forward, not driven by fear, but led by faith.

As a couple, trusting God together strengthens your unity. It invites you to pray over decisions, encourage each other in waiting seasons, and remind each other of God's faithfulness when one of you feels unsure. It turns your relationship into a partnership with God at the center, not just between yourselves.

This week, name your hopes and fears. Lay them at Jesus' feet. Commit your way to Him—your decisions, your family, your finances, your calling, your health. Then walk forward together, hand in hand, knowing the God who holds your future also holds you.

PSALM TO MEDITATE ON

"Many are the plans in a person's heart, but it is the Lord's purpose that prevails."—Proverbs 19:21 (NIV)

GUIDED MEDITATION ON THE PSALM

Read Proverbs 19 slowly and reflectively.

Ask together:

- ﺱ Lord, what of our plans do You want to bless, reshape, or redirect?
- ﺱ How can we rest in Your purposes, even when we don't yet see the full picture?

Picture yourselves walking a road hand in hand, with Jesus walking beside you, leading the way.

DECLARATIONS FOR THE WEEK

We declare:

- ی Our future is in God's loving and powerful hands.
- ی We trust Him to guide our steps and shape our days.
- ی We surrender anxiety and control and walk forward in peace.
- ی We face the future together, anchored in God's promises.

God's purpose for our marriage is good, beautiful, and unfolding in His time.

COMMUNION PRAYER

(Prepare bread (or a cracker) and a small cup of juice. Together, hold the bread and pray).

Lord Jesus Christ, we come before You now, humbled and grateful. You are the Bread of Life, the true Manna from heaven. You gave Your body to be broken for us, that we might be made whole—spirit, soul, and body. You poured out Your blood as the cup of the new covenant, that we might be cleansed, forgiven, and reconciled to God.

We pause to remember Your sacrifice. We remember Your wounds, Your love, Your victory. We remember that You carried our sickness, our grief, our sins, and our shame upon Yourself at the cross (see

Isaiah 53:4–5). You conquered death, hell, and the grave, and You rose again, so that we might share in Your life.

We confess, Lord, that we need You. We bring before You every place in our lives and marriage where we are weak, divided, hurting, or burdened. We ask for Your forgiveness for where we have spoken in anger, withheld love, carried resentment, or failed to honor one another. Wash us clean, Jesus—in Your mercy, cover us with Your righteousness.

As we eat this bread, we receive Your healing. Heal our hearts where they are wounded. Heal our minds where they are anxious or tormented. Heal our bodies where they are sick or weak. Heal our marriage where it has been strained or broken. Let the same power that raised You from the dead now flow through us. Jesus, You are the Alpha and the Omega, the Beginning and the End. You hold time, eternity, and every detail of our lives. As we eat this bread, we remember Your body—given for us to walk free.

(Eat the bread)

As we drink this cup, we renew our covenant with You and with each other. We declare that we are Yours, and You are ours. We belong to You—as individuals and as a couple. Strengthen the bond between us. Let our love be patient, kind, humble, and enduring. Let forgiveness flow freely in our home. Let Your peace reign over our household. Jesus, thank You for Your blood, poured out for forgiveness and new life. As we drink this cup, we receive Your blood—sealing us in a covenant of love, grace, and hope.

(Drink the cup)

Jesus, fill us with Your Spirit. Unite us in Your love. Draw us deeper into the mystery of union with You—that we may be one as You and the Father are one. Teach us to love one another with Your supernatural love. Teach us to walk in Your ways. Teach us to see our marriage not only as partnership, but as a holy vessel that carries Your glory into this world.

We receive now—with faith and joy—the blessings You have promised. Blessings of peace, healing, provision, restoration, protection, wisdom, and overflowing grace. We stand in agreement, as one, declaring that no weapon formed against us shall prosper. We break every assignment of the enemy against our lives and marriage. We release blessing over our future, over our family, and over the generations to come.

We give You our future: our hopes, our fears, our unknowns. Lead us, Lord. Shape us. Carry us. Make us faithful as we follow You, together.

Thank You, Jesus. Amen.

FINAL WORD

You don't have to figure out everything ahead—you only need to trust the One who goes before you. Step forward this week with hands open, hearts united, and eyes fixed on the God who is writing your story.

COUPLES ACTIVITY: "THE FUTURE SURRENDER PRAYER"

Set aside time this week to sit together and each answer:

- ی What's one hope I carry for our future?
- ی What's one fear or uncertainty I need to surrender?

Write them down or speak them aloud. Then pray together: *"Lord, we place these hopes and fears into Your hands. Lead us, guide us, and help us trust You with all we are and all we will become. Amen."*

WEEK 34
GRATITUDE FOR GROWTH—
CELEBRATING HOW FAR WE'VE COME

MEDITATION SCRIPTURES

"Being confident of this, that He who began a good work in you will carry it on to completion until the day of Christ Jesus."—Philippians 1:6 (NIV)

"You shall remember the whole way that the Lord your God has led you."—Deuteronomy 8:2 (ESV)

"Give thanks to the Lord, for He is good! His faithful love endures forever."—Psalm 107:1 (NLT)

GUIDED MEDITATION ON SCRIPTURE

Sit together quietly, maybe resting close or holding hands.

Read the scriptures aloud slowly. Let the words *good work... remember the way... give thanks... faithful love* settle deeply into your spirit.

Reflect silently:

- ی Where have we grown as individuals and as a couple in this past season?
- ی What challenges have we faced—and how has God been faithful to lead us through?
- ی What small or big victories can we stop and thank God for right now?

Sit in quiet gratitude, letting your heart fill with thanksgiving.

QUOTE FOR TODAY

"Do not disdain the small beginnings of grace; for in every small step, God's infinite love is present, and it leads you ever forward."
—St. Francis de Sales

WORD FOR THE WEEK

It's easy to rush through life without noticing how far God has brought you. You move from one challenge to the next, one goal to another, and forget to stop and marvel at the grace that has shaped your journey. But gratitude for growth is vital—it humbles you, encourages you, and anchors you in the goodness of God.

As a couple, you have likely weathered storms, navigated changes, healed wounds, and deepened love in ways you couldn't have imagined at the start. Maybe you've become better listeners, more patient, more forgiving, more resilient, more united. These are holy victories, even if they came through struggle.

Scripture invites us to remember the way the Lord has led us—to trace His faithfulness, name His mercies, and give thanks. This isn't about pretending everything has been easy; it's about recognizing that God has been present and active in every step, turning even hardships into places of growth.

This week, pause and reflect. Celebrate how far you've come—not because you've arrived, but because God is faithfully, patiently, lovingly completing His work in you. Gratitude turns the journey itself into worship.

PSALM TO MEDITATE ON

"The Lord has done great things for us, and we are filled with joy."—Psalm 126:3 (NIV)

GUIDED MEDITATION ON THE PSALM

Read Psalm 126:3 aloud slowly.

Ask together:

- Lord, what "great things" have You done in our lives, even in small or hidden ways?
- Where do we need to pause and say, *"Thank You"*?

Picture yourselves looking back over the road you've walked, seeing God's hand in places you might have missed.

DECLARATIONS FOR THE WEEK

We declare:

- ی God has been faithful to us every step of the way.
- ی We give thanks for the growth, healing, and love He has worked in us.
- ی We celebrate how far we've come, even as we trust Him for what's ahead.
- ی Our marriage is a living testimony of God's transforming grace.

We walk forward with joy, hope, and gratitude.

COMMUNION PRAYER

(Prepare bread (or a cracker) and a small cup of juice. Together, hold the bread and pray).

Lord Jesus Christ, we come before You now, humbled and grateful. You are the Bread of Life, the true Manna from heaven. You gave Your body to be broken for us, that we might be made whole—spirit, soul, and body. You poured out Your blood as the cup of the new covenant, that we might be cleansed, forgiven, and reconciled to God.

We pause to remember Your sacrifice. We remember Your wounds, Your love, Your victory. We remember that You carried our sickness, our grief, our sins, and our shame upon Yourself at the cross (see Isaiah 53:4–5). You conquered death, hell, and the grave, and You rose again, so that we might share in Your life.

We confess, Lord, that we need You. We bring before You every place in our lives and marriage where we are weak, divided, hurting, or burdened. We ask for Your forgiveness for where we have spoken in anger, withheld love, carried resentment, or failed to honor one another. Wash us clean, Jesus—in Your mercy, cover us with Your righteousness.

As we eat this bread, we receive Your healing. Heal our hearts where they are wounded. Heal our minds where they are anxious or tormented. Heal our bodies where they are sick or weak. Heal our marriage where it has been strained or broken. Let the same power that raised You from the dead now flow through us. Jesus, You have walked every step with us—through laughter, through tears, through change, through growth. Thank You for Your faithfulness. As we eat this bread, we remember Your body—given to redeem every part of our journey.

(Eat the bread)

As we drink this cup, we renew our covenant with You and with each other. We declare that we are Yours, and You are ours. We belong to You—as individuals and as a couple. Strengthen the bond between us. Let our love be patient, kind, humble, and enduring. Let forgiveness flow freely in our home. Let Your peace reign over our household. Jesus, thank You for Your blood, poured out for forgiveness and new life. As we drink this cup, we receive Your blood—poured out to transform and renew us.

(Drink the cup)

Jesus, fill us with Your Spirit. Unite us in Your love. Draw us deeper into the mystery of union with You—that we may be one as You and the Father are one. Teach us to love one another with Your supernatural love. Teach us to walk in Your ways. Teach us to see our marriage not only as partnership, but as a holy vessel that carries Your glory into this world.

We receive now—with faith and joy—the blessings You have promised. Blessings of peace, healing, provision, restoration, protection, wisdom, and overflowing grace. We stand in agreement, as one, declaring that no weapon formed against us shall prosper. We break every assignment of the enemy against our lives and marriage. We release blessing over our future, over our family, and over the generations to come.

We pause to say, Thank You, Lord. Thank You for what You have done. Thank You for what You are doing. Thank You for what You will do. We trust You, and we are grateful.

Thank You, Jesus. Amen.

FINAL WORD

Every step forward matters. Every small change counts. Let this be a week of joyful reflection, where you look back with gratitude and forward with hope, knowing God is not finished with you yet.

COUPLES ACTIVITY: "OUR JOURNEY OF THANKS"

Set aside 30 minutes this week to reflect and share:

- What are three ways we've seen each other grow?
- What has God done in our marriage that we're grateful for?
- What challenge did we come through that made us stronger?

Write these down or speak them out loud. Then pray together: *"Lord, thank You for how You've led us. Help us to keep growing, loving, and trusting You. Amen."*

WEEK 35
FINDING JOY IN THE PRESENT— SAVORING TODAY TOGETHER

MEDITATION SCRIPTURES

"This is the day the Lord has made; we will rejoice and be glad in it."—Psalm 118:24 (NKJV)

"Do not worry about tomorrow, for tomorrow will worry about its own things. Sufficient for the day is its own trouble."— Matthew 6:34 (NKJV)

"Taste and see that the Lord is good; blessed is the one who takes refuge in Him."—Psalm 34:8 (NIV)

GUIDED MEDITATION ON SCRIPTURE

Sit quietly together, maybe in the early morning or evening.

Read the scriptures aloud slowly. Let the words *this is the day... do not worry... taste and see* settle deep into your hearts.

Reflect silently:

ᔑ Where do we tend to live—in the past, the future, or the present?

- ي How can we slow down and savor God's gifts in this day?
- ي What simple moments bring us joy when we're fully present?

Sit for a few moments just breathing, noticing the beauty and goodness around you.

QUOTE FOR TODAY

"God is in the present moment, and if we are not present, we miss Him."

—*Brother Lawrence*

WORD FOR THE WEEK

Marriage is lived not in grand milestones, but in thousands of ordinary moments—quiet breakfasts, shared glances, small laughs, passing prayers. And yet, so often we rush past these moments, distracted by past regrets or future worries, missing the gifts right in front of us.

Scripture invites us to rejoice today, trust today, taste and see God's goodness today. Tomorrow has its own burdens, yesterday its own lessons, but right now is where joy is waiting.

For couples, this means learning to pause: to savor a meal without phones, to take a walk and notice the sky, to listen to each other without agenda, to laugh freely, to thank God for a day well-lived. These small acts build a deep, lasting joy—the kind that weathers storms and creates a home of peace.

This week, ask God to help you live here, not just in your plans or pressures. Joy is not something you chase down the road; it's something you unwrap today, together, in His presence.

PSALM TO MEDITATE ON

"You make known to me the path of life; in Your presence there is fullness of joy; at Your right hand are pleasures forevermore."—Psalm 16:11 (ESV)

GUIDED MEDITATION ON THE PSALM

Read Psalm 16:11 slowly, maybe even twice.

Ask together:

- ی Lord, where are You inviting us to experience joy right now?
- ی How can we slow down to notice and receive the pleasures You've placed in today?

Picture yourselves walking with God through today, hands open, hearts light.

DECLARATIONS FOR THE WEEK

We declare:

- ی We choose joy today—not waiting for everything to be perfect.

- ی We release past regrets and future worries into God's hands.
- ی We savor the small, ordinary gifts of love, laughter, and presence.
- ی God is with us today, here, now, and His joy strengthens us.

Our home is a place of gratitude, wonder, and delight.

COMMUNION PRAYER

(Prepare bread (or a cracker) and a small cup of juice. Together, hold the bread and pray).

Lord Jesus Christ, we come before You now, humbled and grateful. You are the Bread of Life, the true Manna from heaven. You gave Your body to be broken for us, that we might be made whole—spirit, soul, and body. You poured out Your blood as the cup of the new covenant, that we might be cleansed, forgiven, and reconciled to God.

We pause to remember Your sacrifice. We remember Your wounds, Your love, Your victory. We remember that You carried our sickness, our grief, our sins, and our shame upon Yourself at the cross (see Isaiah 53:4–5). You conquered death, hell, and the grave, and You rose again, so that we might share in Your life.

We confess, Lord, that we need You. We bring before You every place in our lives and marriage where we are weak, divided, hurting, or burdened. We ask for Your forgiveness for where we have spoken in anger, withheld love, carried resentment, or failed to honor one another. Wash us clean, Jesus—in Your mercy, cover us with Your righteousness.

As we eat this bread, we receive Your healing. Heal our hearts where they are wounded. Heal our minds where they are anxious or tormented. Heal our bodies where they are sick or weak. Heal our marriage where it has been strained or broken. Let the same power that raised You from the dead now flow through us. Jesus, You are not only our hope for tomorrow; You are our joy for today. You meet us here, now, in this moment. As we eat this bread, we taste and see that You are good.

(Eat the bread)

As we drink this cup, we renew our covenant with You and with each other. We declare that we are Yours, and You are ours. We belong to You—as individuals and as a couple. Strengthen the bond between us. Let our love be patient, kind, humble, and enduring. Let forgiveness flow freely in our home. Let Your peace reign over our household. Jesus, thank You for Your blood, poured out for forgiveness and new life. As we drink this cup, we remember that Your love is present, faithful, and sufficient.

(Drink the cup)

Jesus, fill us with Your Spirit. Unite us in Your love. Draw us deeper into the mystery of union with You—that we may be one as You and the Father are one. Teach us to love one another with Your supernatural love. Teach us to walk in Your ways. Teach us to see our marriage not only as partnership, but as a holy vessel that carries Your glory into this world.

We receive now—with faith and joy—the blessings You have promised. Blessings of peace, healing, provision, restoration, protection, wisdom, and overflowing grace. We stand in agreement, as one, declaring that no weapon formed against us shall prosper. We break every assignment of the enemy against our lives and marriage. We release blessing over our future, over our family, and over the generations to come.

Help us slow down, Lord. Help us laugh, notice, thank, and cherish each other today. Fill our hearts with quiet delight in You and in the life You've given us.

Thank You, Jesus. Amen.

FINAL WORD

Joy isn't found in perfect circumstances—it's found in present grace. Open your eyes this week. Look for it. Receive it. And rejoice, together.

COUPLES ACTIVITY: "THE JOY JAR"

This week, set out a small jar or bowl. Each day, both of you write down one small joy you noticed:

- ﺱ A moment of laughter.
- ﺱ A good meal.

ى A kind word.

ى A prayer answered.

At the end of the week, sit together, read them aloud, and thank God: *"Lord, You were with us in all these moments. Thank You."*

WEEK 36
WORSHIPING TOGETHER—LIFTING ONE VOICE, ONE HEART

MEDITATION SCRIPTURES

"Oh, magnify the Lord with me, and let us exalt His name together."—Psalm 34:3 (NKJV)

"For where two or three are gathered in My name, I am there in the midst of them."—Matthew 18:20 (NKJV)

"Sing to the Lord with grateful praise; make music to our God."—Psalm 147:7 (NIV)

GUIDED MEDITATION ON SCRIPTURE

Sit quietly together. Maybe hold hands or rest in stillness beside each other.

Read the scriptures aloud slowly. Let the words *magnify... exalt... together... sing... grateful praise* stir your spirit.

Reflect silently:

- ﺱ When was the last time we worshiped God together—outside of church, just the two of us?

ৎ How might worship strengthen our marriage, soften our hearts, or bring joy into our home?

ৎ What simple ways can we bring worship into our daily rhythm?

Take a deep breath, imagining your hearts lifting in unity before God.

QUOTE FOR TODAY

"The soul that sings to God opens itself like a flower to the sun— and both are changed in the warmth of His love."
—St. Hildegard of Bingen

WORD FOR THE WEEK

Worship is more than singing—it's a posture of the heart, a lifting of the soul toward God in love, awe, and gratitude. But something unique and powerful happens when a couple worships together: walls soften, hearts unite, and God's presence fills the space between them.

Many couples pray together, but few worship together outside of church. Yet worship at home—through music, thanksgiving, Scripture, or simple words of praise—invites God to reign not just over your Sunday, but over your everyday. It reminds you that you are not just partners in life, but co-worshipers before the King.

Worship breaks heaviness. It shifts focus from problems to promises, from exhaustion to renewal, from isolation to connection. It creates a rhythm of gratitude, wonder, and love. And it deepens your awareness of God's goodness in your marriage, especially in hard or dry seasons.

This week, take simple steps to worship together. Play a worship song while you cook, pause to thank God aloud, read a Psalm of praise, or sit in quiet awe of His beauty. It doesn't have to be formal or long—just real, offered in love.

PSALM TO MEDITATE ON

"Let everything that has breath praise the Lord. Praise the Lord!"—Psalm 150:6 (NKJV)

GUIDED MEDITATION ON THE PSALM

Read Psalm 150:6 aloud slowly, maybe even more than once.

Ask together:

- ی Lord, how can we praise You together in this season—with our words, our hearts, our home?
- ی What happens in us and between us when we worship You as one?

Picture your marriage like an instrument in God's hands, offering a song of love and gratitude.

DECLARATIONS FOR THE WEEK

We declare:

- ی Our marriage is a place of worship, not just work.
- ی We lift our voices and hearts to God together.
- ی God's presence fills our home with peace, joy, and love.

- Worship strengthens our bond and refreshes our spirits.
- We will praise God in every season—together.

COMMUNION PRAYER

**(Prepare bread (or a cracker) and a small cup of juice.
Together, hold the bread and pray).**

Lord Jesus Christ, we come before You now, humbled and grateful. You are the Bread of Life, the true Manna from heaven. You gave Your body to be broken for us, that we might be made whole—spirit, soul, and body. You poured out Your blood as the cup of the new covenant, that we might be cleansed, forgiven, and reconciled to God.

We pause to remember Your sacrifice. We remember Your wounds, Your love, Your victory. We remember that You carried our sickness, our grief, our sins, and our shame upon Yourself at the cross (see Isaiah 53:4–5). You conquered death, hell, and the grave, and You rose again, so that we might share in Your life.

We confess, Lord, that we need You. We bring before You every place in our lives and marriage where we are weak, divided, hurting, or burdened. We ask for Your forgiveness for where we have spoken in anger, withheld love, carried resentment, or failed to honor one another. Wash us clean, Jesus—in Your mercy, cover us with Your righteousness.

As we eat this bread, we receive Your healing. Heal our hearts where they are wounded. Heal our minds where they are anxious or tormented. Heal our bodies where they are sick or weak. Heal our marriage where it has been strained or broken. Let the same power that raised You from the dead now flow through us. Jesus, You are worthy of all our praise—in the highs, in the lows, in the ordinary days between. You are our joy, our peace, and our reason to sing. As we eat this bread, we remember Your body, given in love.

(Eat the bread)

As we drink this cup, we renew our covenant with You and with each other. We declare that we are Yours, and You are ours. We belong to You—as individuals and as a couple. Strengthen the bond between us. Let our love be patient, kind, humble, and enduring. Let forgiveness flow freely in our home. Let Your peace reign over our household. Jesus, thank You for Your blood, poured out for forgiveness and new life. As we drink this cup, we receive Your blood, poured out to bring us into communion with You.

(Drink the cup)

Jesus, fill us with Your Spirit. Unite us in Your love. Draw us deeper into the mystery of union with You—that we may be one as You and the Father are one. Teach us to love one another with Your supernatural love. Teach us to walk in Your ways. Teach us to see our marriage not only as partnership, but as a holy vessel that carries Your glory into this world.

We receive now—with faith and joy—the blessings You have promised. Blessings of peace, healing, provision, restoration, protection, wisdom, and overflowing grace. We stand in agreement, as one, declaring that no weapon formed against us shall prosper. We break every assignment of the enemy against our lives and marriage. We release blessing over our future, over our family, and over the generations to come.

We lift our voices and hearts to You, together. Be glorified in our love, in our home, in our worship. Let our marriage be a song that pleases You.

Thank You, Jesus. Amen.

FINAL WORD

Worship transforms everything it touches—your heart, your home, your marriage. Make space this week for praise, and watch how God meets you in beauty, joy, and strength.

COUPLES ACTIVITY: "OUR WORSHIP MOMENT"

This week, choose one simple way to worship together:

- ও Play a favorite worship song and sing or listen together.
- ও Read aloud a Psalm of praise (like Psalm 100 or 145).
- ও Share one reason you're grateful to God today.
- ও End the day by saying aloud: *"We praise You, Lord, for Your goodness."*

At the end of the week, reflect: *"How did worship change our atmosphere? Our hearts? Our connection?"*

WEEK 37
RESTING TOGETHER—FINDING RENEWAL AS ONE

MEDITATION SCRIPTURES

"Come to Me, all you who labor and are heavy laden, and I will give you rest."—Matthew 11:28 (NKJV)

"In peace I will lie down and sleep, for You alone, Lord, make me dwell in safety."—Psalm 4:8 (NIV)

"There remains, then, a Sabbath-rest for the people of God."—Hebrews 4:9 (NIV)

GUIDED MEDITATION ON SCRIPTURE

Sit quietly together, maybe dim the lights or set a peaceful atmosphere.

Read the scriptures aloud slowly. Let the words *come to Me... give you rest... peace... safety... Sabbath-rest* calm your minds and settle your hearts.

Reflect silently:

- Where are we carrying weariness in our lives or relationship?
- How might we practice rest—not just physically, but emotionally and spiritually—together?
- What does God want to restore in us this season?

Take a deep breath together, inviting God's peace to surround you.

QUOTE FOR TODAY

"To rest in God is to be carried by His love, not driven by our striving."

—*Thomas à Kempis*

WORD FOR THE WEEK

Many couples live in a constant state of hurry, pressure, and exhaustion. Work demands, family needs, ministry, health challenges, or financial stress can drain joy and connection, leaving little space for rest. But rest is not laziness—it's a holy rhythm God invites us into for renewal, delight, and intimacy.

Rest is where bodies recover, minds quiet, hearts reconnect, and souls remember they are loved. When you rest together—whether through a peaceful walk, quiet prayer, a shared meal, or simply slowing down the pace—you are creating space for God to restore what daily life drains.

Learning to rest together means being intentional. It means saying no sometimes, protecting downtime, unplugging, and choosing presence over productivity. It means listening to what your body, marriage, and soul need, and trusting God to meet you in stillness.

This week, invite God to lead you into His rest—not just as individuals, but as a couple. Let rest become not just a break, but a gift of renewal and communion with Him and each other.

PSALM TO MEDITATE ON

"The Lord is my shepherd; I shall not want. He makes me to lie down in green pastures; He leads me beside the still waters. He restores my soul."—Psalm 23:1–3 (NKJV)

GUIDED MEDITATION ON THE PSALM

Read Psalm 23:1-3 slowly, savoring each line.

Ask together:

- ﺱ Lord, where do You want to lead us into green pastures and still waters?
- ﺱ What kind of rest do we most need this week—in body, heart, mind, or spirit?

Picture God as your Shepherd, gently guiding you to places of peace and restoration.

DECLARATIONS FOR THE WEEK

We declare:

- ⨝ God invites us to rest and restores our souls.
- ⨝ We make space for rest in our marriage and home.
- ⨝ We release pressure and striving, and we receive God's peace.
- ⨝ Our rest is a gift to each other and a reflection of trust in God.
- ⨝ We are renewed, refreshed, and reconnected in Christ.

COMMUNION PRAYER

(Prepare bread (or a cracker) and a small cup of juice. Together, hold the bread and pray).

Lord Jesus Christ, we come before You now, humbled and grateful. You are the Bread of Life, the true Manna from heaven. You gave Your body to be broken for us, that we might be made whole—spirit, soul, and body. You poured out Your blood as the cup of the new covenant, that we might be cleansed, forgiven, and reconciled to God.

We pause to remember Your sacrifice. We remember Your wounds, Your love, Your victory. We remember that You carried our sickness, our grief, our sins, and our shame upon Yourself at the cross (see Isaiah 53:4–5). You conquered death, hell, and the grave, and You rose again, so that we might share in Your life.

We confess, Lord, that we need You. We bring before You every place in our lives and marriage where we are weak, divided, hurting, or burdened. We ask for Your forgiveness for where we have spoken in anger, withheld love, carried resentment, or failed to honor one another. Wash us clean, Jesus—in Your mercy, cover us with Your righteousness.

As we eat this bread, we receive Your healing. Heal our hearts where they are wounded. Heal our minds where they are anxious or tormented. Heal our bodies where they are sick or weak. Heal our marriage where it has been strained or broken. Let the same power that raised You from the dead now flow through us. Jesus, You are our rest. You invite us to come to You, lay down our burdens, and receive peace. You restore what we cannot restore ourselves. As we eat this bread, we remember Your body—given to carry our burdens.

(Eat the bread)

As we drink this cup, we renew our covenant with You and with each other. We declare that we are Yours, and You are ours. We belong to You—as individuals and as a couple. Strengthen the bond between us. Let our love be patient, kind, humble, and enduring. Let forgiveness flow freely in our home. Let Your peace reign over our household. Jesus, thank You for Your blood, poured out for forgiveness and new life. As we drink this cup, we receive Your blood—poured out to bring us into perfect peace.

(Drink the cup)

Jesus, fill us with Your Spirit. Unite us in Your love. Draw us deeper into the mystery of union with You—that we may be one as You and the Father are one. Teach us to love one another with Your supernatural love. Teach us to walk in Your ways. Teach us to see our marriage not only as partnership, but as a holy vessel that carries Your glory into this world.

We receive now—with faith and joy—the blessings You have promised. Blessings of peace, healing, provision, restoration, protection, wisdom, and overflowing grace. We stand in agreement, as one, declaring that no weapon formed against us shall prosper. We break every assignment of the enemy against our lives and marriage. We release blessing over our future, over our family, and over the generations to come.

We release our striving, our exhaustion, our fears. We receive Your rest, Your renewal, and Your love. Teach us to rest well—with You and with each other.

Thank You, Jesus. Amen.

FINAL WORD

Rest is not optional for a healthy marriage—it's essential. Let this be a week where you slow down, draw close, and let God fill the spaces you've been trying to fill with busyness.

COUPLES ACTIVITY: "SABBATH HOUR TOGETHER"

Pick one hour this week to practice rest together.

- No chores, no screens, no work talk.
- Sit outside, take a slow walk, share a quiet meal, listen to music, or rest side by side.
- Let it be an hour of just being—with each other and with God.

At the end, thank God aloud: *"Lord, thank You for rest, for love, and for this time together. Help us carry Your peace into the days ahead."*

WEEK 38
HANDLING CONFLICT WITH GRACE—FIGHTING FOR, NOT AGAINST, EACH OTHER

MEDITATION SCRIPTURES

"A soft answer turns away wrath, but a harsh word stirs up anger."—Proverbs 15:1 (NKJV)

"Be kind to one another, tenderhearted, forgiving one another, as God in Christ forgave you."—Ephesians 4:32 (ESV)

"Understand this, my dear brothers and sisters: You must all be quick to listen, slow to speak, and slow to get angry."—James 1:19 (NLT)

GUIDED MEDITATION ON SCRIPTURE

Sit together quietly, perhaps after a calm moment or in a time of reflection.

Read the scriptures aloud slowly. Let the words *soft answer... tenderhearted... quick to listen... slow to anger* settle over you.

Reflect silently:

- How do we typically handle conflict—with grace, or with tension?
- What old patterns might God want to soften or heal?
- How can we become better at listening, forgiving, and working through hard things as a team?

Invite God to show you one small shift that could bring more peace to your conflict moments.

QUOTE FOR TODAY

"Where there is humility, there is peace; where there is love, there is the quieting of all storms."

—*St. Francis of Assisi*

WORD FOR THE WEEK

Every couple faces conflict—it's part of being two unique people sharing one life. But conflict doesn't have to destroy connection; it can actually deepen love when handled with grace. The goal is not avoiding disagreement, but learning to disagree in a way that honors God and each other.

Healthy conflict requires humility: the courage to say, *"I was wrong,"* or *"I'm sorry,"* and the tenderness to say, *"I forgive you."* It means pausing before harsh words, choosing to listen before defending, and remembering that you are on the same team.

God calls couples to be peacemakers, not peace-fakers—not pretending everything's fine, but seeking real healing, even when it's hard. This takes practice, prayer, and often repentance. But as you learn to handle conflict with grace, your marriage becomes stronger, softer, and more secure.

This week, ask God to help you notice how you handle tension. Invite Him into your disagreements, big or small, and let Him guide you to be quick to listen, slow to speak, and rich in love.

PSALM TO MEDITATE ON

"Turn from evil and do good; seek peace and pursue it."—Psalm 34:14 (NIV)

GUIDED MEDITATION ON THE PSALM

Read Psalm 34:14 slowly.

Ask together:

- Lord, where do we need to pursue peace more intentionally in our marriage?
- What step can we take toward more grace-filled communication?

Picture God planting peace like a seed in your home—one you will tend together.

DECLARATIONS FOR THE WEEK

We declare:

- We are on the same team, fighting for our marriage, not against each other.
- We are quick to listen, slow to speak, and slow to anger.
- We handle conflict with humility, patience, and love.
- God helps us grow through disagreements, not be divided by them.
- Our marriage is a place of grace, healing, and peace.

COMMUNION PRAYER

(Prepare bread (or a cracker) and a small cup of juice. Together, hold the bread and pray).

Lord Jesus Christ, we come before You now, humbled and grateful. You are the Bread of Life, the true Manna from heaven. You gave Your body to be broken for us, that we might be made whole—spirit, soul, and body. You poured out Your blood as the cup of the new covenant, that we might be cleansed, forgiven, and reconciled to God.

We pause to remember Your sacrifice. We remember Your wounds, Your love, Your victory. We remember that You carried our sickness, our grief, our sins, and our shame upon Yourself at the cross (see Isaiah 53:4–5). You conquered death, hell, and the grave, and You rose again, so that we might share in Your life.

We confess, Lord, that we need You. We bring before You every place in our lives and marriage where we are weak, divided, hurting, or burdened. We ask for Your forgiveness for where we have spoken in anger, withheld love, carried resentment, or failed to honor one another. Wash us clean, Jesus—in Your mercy, cover us with Your righteousness.

As we eat this bread, we receive Your healing. Heal our hearts where they are wounded. Heal our minds where they are anxious or tormented. Heal our bodies where they are sick or weak. Heal our marriage where it has been strained or broken. Let the same power that raised You from the dead now flow through us. Jesus, You are the Prince of Peace. You bring healing where we are hurt, unity where we are divided, and love where we are hardened. As we eat this bread, we remember Your body—broken to make us whole.

(Eat the bread)

As we drink this cup, we renew our covenant with You and with each other. We declare that we are Yours, and You are ours. We belong to You—as individuals and as a couple. Strengthen the bond between us. Let our love be patient, kind, humble, and enduring. Let forgiveness flow freely in our home. Let Your peace reign over our household. Jesus, thank You for Your blood, poured out for forgiveness and new life. As we drink this cup, we receive Your blood—poured out to reconcile us to God and to each other.

(Drink the cup)

Jesus, fill us with Your Spirit. Unite us in Your love. Draw us deeper into the mystery of union with You—that we may be one as You and the Father are one. Teach us to love one another with Your supernatural love. Teach us to walk in Your ways. Teach us to see our marriage not only as partnership, but as a holy vessel that carries Your glory into this world.

We receive now—with faith and joy—the blessings You have promised. Blessings of peace, healing, provision, restoration, protection, wisdom, and overflowing grace. We stand in agreement, as one, declaring that no weapon formed against us shall prosper. We break every assignment of the enemy against our lives and marriage. We release blessing over our future, over our family, and over the generations to come.

We invite You into our conflicts, our wounds, our miscommunications. Teach us to forgive, to listen, to speak gently, and to love deeply. Make our marriage a reflection of Your peace.

Thank You, Jesus. Amen.

FINAL WORD

Conflict is not the enemy—disconnection is. Let this week be a time where you fight not to win against each other, but to win each other's hearts again and again.

COUPLES ACTIVITY: "THE GRACE CHECK-IN"

Set aside time this week to gently ask each other:

- How do you feel we handle conflict?
- What helps you feel safe and heard when we disagree?
- What's one way we can both improve at resolving tensions with love?

Pray together: *"Lord, help us be quick to listen, slow to speak, and eager to love, even in hard moments."*

WEEK 39
HEALING FROM PAST WOUNDS— WALKING THE PATH OF RESTORATION TOGETHER

MEDITATION SCRIPTURES

"He heals the brokenhearted and binds up their wounds."—Psalm 147:3 (NKJV)

"Forget the former things; do not dwell on the past. See, I am doing a new thing! Now it springs up; do you not perceive it?"—Isaiah 43:18–19 (NIV)

"Cast all your anxiety on Him because He cares for you."—1 Peter 5:7 (NIV)

GUIDED MEDITATION ON SCRIPTURE

Sit quietly together, perhaps holding hands or resting in stillness.

Read the scriptures aloud slowly. Let the words *Heals... binds up... do not dwell... new thing... He cares* flow over your hearts.

Reflect silently:

- Are there past wounds—from before or within our marriage—that still shape how we love, trust, or communicate?
- Where do we need God's healing touch, either individually or as a couple?
- What *"new thing"* might God want to do in us as we walk this healing path?

Sit quietly, imagining God's love as a gentle light shining into any place of pain.

QUOTE FOR TODAY

"The soul is healed by being with God and letting His love touch what hurts."

—*Julian of Norwich*

WORD FOR THE WEEK

Every marriage carries some measure of past pain. Maybe it's wounds from childhood, past relationships, betrayals, losses, or even old hurts between you. Left unhealed, these wounds can quietly shape how you relate: how you trust, how you react, how you withdraw or reach out.

But the good news of the gospel is this: Jesus is a healer. He comes not only to forgive sins but to restore broken hearts, to bind up wounds, and to make all things new. Healing is not about pretending the past didn't happen; it's about letting God transform its hold on you, so you are no longer defined or limited by it.

For couples, healing often begins with gentle honesty: naming what hurts, listening without judgment, and bringing these wounds before God together. It may take time, patience, and sometimes outside help (pastoral care, counselling, or support), but every step is holy ground when you invite God into it.

This week, don't rush to fix everything. Simply take one step toward healing—whether that's a conversation, a prayer, a letter, or an act of forgiveness. Trust that God's love is strong enough to carry you both.

PSALM TO MEDITATE ON

"The Lord is close to the brokenhearted and saves those who are crushed in spirit."—Psalm 34:18 (NIV)

GUIDED MEDITATION ON THE PSALM

Read Psalm 34:18 slowly, maybe more than once.

Ask together:

- ﮮ Lord, where are You inviting us to experience Your nearness in our broken or tender places?
- ﮮ What part of our story do You want to bring healing and hope to?

Picture Jesus drawing close, not rushing you, just being with you, ready to help carry what's heavy.

DECLARATIONS FOR THE WEEK

We declare:

- ও God is our healer, and His love restores what is broken.
- ও We are not defined by past wounds; we are defined by God's grace.
- ও We walk together on the path of restoration, hand in hand.
- ও We offer each other patience, kindness, and compassion.
- ও Our marriage is a story of healing, hope, and new beginnings.

COMMUNION PRAYER

(Prepare bread (or a cracker) and a small cup of juice. Together, hold the bread and pray).

Lord Jesus Christ, we come before You now, humbled and grateful. You are the Bread of Life, the true Manna from heaven. You gave Your body to be broken for us, that we might be made whole—spirit, soul, and body. You poured out Your blood as the cup of the new covenant, that we might be cleansed, forgiven, and reconciled to God.

We pause to remember Your sacrifice. We remember Your wounds, Your love, Your victory. We remember that You carried our sickness, our grief, our sins, and our shame upon Yourself at the cross (see

Isaiah 53:4–5). You conquered death, hell, and the grave, and You rose again, so that we might share in Your life.

We confess, Lord, that we need You. We bring before You every place in our lives and marriage where we are weak, divided, hurting, or burdened. We ask for Your forgiveness for where we have spoken in anger, withheld love, carried resentment, or failed to honor one another. Wash us clean, Jesus—in Your mercy, cover us with Your righteousness.

As we eat this bread, we receive Your healing. Heal our hearts where they are wounded. Heal our minds where they are anxious or tormented. Heal our bodies where they are sick or weak. Heal our marriage where it has been strained or broken. Let the same power that raised You from the dead now flow through us. Jesus, You bore our wounds so we might be healed. You carried our sorrows so we could walk in joy. You entered our brokenness to make us whole. As we eat this bread, we remember Your body—given for our healing.

(Eat the bread)

As we drink this cup, we renew our covenant with You and with each other. We declare that we are Yours, and You are ours. We belong to You—as individuals and as a couple. Strengthen the bond between us. Let our love be patient, kind, humble, and enduring. Let forgiveness flow freely in our home. Let Your peace reign over our household. Jesus, thank You for Your blood, poured out for forgiveness and new life. As we drink this cup, we receive Your blood—poured out to restore us to life.

(Drink the cup)

Jesus, fill us with Your Spirit. Unite us in Your love. Draw us deeper into the mystery of union with You—that we may be one as You and the Father are one. Teach us to love one another with Your supernatural love. Teach us to walk in Your ways. Teach us to see our marriage not only as partnership, but as a holy vessel that carries Your glory into this world.

We receive now—with faith and joy—the blessings You have promised. Blessings of peace, healing, provision, restoration, protection, wisdom, and overflowing grace. We stand in agreement, as one, declaring that no weapon formed against us shall prosper. We break every assignment of the enemy against our lives and marriage. We release blessing over our future, over our family, and over the generations to come.

We bring You our past, our pain, our fears. We receive Your love, Your mercy, and Your healing. Make us whole, Lord—as individuals and as a couple.

Thank You, Jesus. Amen.

FINAL WORD

Healing is not always fast or easy, but it is always sacred. Take it one gentle step at a time. God is not rushed, and He delights in walking with you as you heal, love, and grow.

COUPLES ACTIVITY: "A STEP TOWARD HEALING"

Set aside quiet time this week to ask:

- ى Is there any past hurt we need to name or acknowledge?
- ى How can we support each other with compassion and patience?
- ى What is one gentle step we can take toward healing—a prayer, an apology, a promise, or simply presence?

End by praying: *"Lord, we invite You into every wound, seen and unseen. Bring Your healing and teach us to walk together in hope."*

WEEK 40
BUILDING RESILIENCE—STANDING STRONG TOGETHER

MEDITATION SCRIPTURES

"Though one may be overpowered, two can defend themselves. A cord of three strands is not quickly broken."—Ecclesiastes 4:12 (NIV)

"We are hard pressed on every side, yet not crushed; we are perplexed, but not in despair."—2 Corinthians 4:8 (NKJV)

"The Lord God is my strength; He will make my feet like deer's feet, and He will make me walk on my high hills."—Habakkuk 3:19 (NKJV)

GUIDED MEDITATION ON SCRIPTURE

Sit quietly together, take a few slow, deep breaths.

Read the scriptures aloud slowly. Let the words *not quickly broken... not crushed... the Lord God is my strength* settle deeply.

Reflect silently:

- ﺱ What challenges have we faced together—and how has God strengthened us through them?
- ﺱ Where are we being stretched now, and how can we stand together with faith?
- ﺱ How can we keep strengthening our *"cord of three strands"*—with God at the center of our marriage?

Rest in the quiet, picturing God wrapping you both in His strength.

QUOTE FOR TODAY

"The soul's strength is not in escaping trial, but in resting in God through it."

—St. John of the Cross

WORD FOR THE WEEK

Resilience isn't about pretending things are easy—it's about choosing to stay rooted, together, in God's strength, even when life is hard. Every marriage will face storms: illness, loss, conflict, stress, disappointment. What matters is not avoiding hardship, but how you stand through it, hand in hand.

God designed marriage to be a partnership where resilience is multiplied. When one is weak, the other can help carry. When both are weary, God becomes the third strand, holding you together. Resilience grows not just from grit, but from grace—learning to lean on each other and on Him.

It's in the hard seasons that love deepens: when you choose forgiveness over resentment, perseverance over escape, prayer over panic. You discover that what holds you is not just human strength, but the unbreakable faithfulness of God.

This week, reflect on the resilience God is building in you—as individuals and as a couple. Thank Him for the strength He has given and ask Him to keep shaping you into a marriage that weathers storms with grace and faith.

PSALM TO MEDITATE ON

"God is our refuge and strength, an ever-present help in trouble."—Psalm 46:1 (NIV)

GUIDED MEDITATION ON THE PSALM

Read Psalm 46:1 slowly, maybe more than once.

Ask together:

- Lord, how have You been our refuge in past storms?
- Where do we need Your strength right now?

Picture your marriage like a tree: deeply rooted, flexible in the wind, anchored in God's unshakable ground.

DECLARATIONS FOR THE WEEK

We declare:

- ی God is our strength, our refuge, and our help.
- ی We face challenges together, not alone.
- ی We are a cord of three strands—united, resilient, unbroken.
- ی Hard times will shape us, not shatter us.
- ی We stand firm in love, faith, and hope.

COMMUNION PRAYER

**(Prepare bread (or a cracker) and a small cup of juice.
Together, hold the bread and pray).**

Lord Jesus Christ, we come before You now, humbled and grateful. You are the Bread of Life, the true Manna from heaven. You gave Your body to be broken for us, that we might be made whole—spirit, soul, and body. You poured out Your blood as the cup of the new covenant, that we might be cleansed, forgiven, and reconciled to God.

We pause to remember Your sacrifice. We remember Your wounds, Your love, Your victory. We remember that You carried our sickness, our grief, our sins, and our shame upon Yourself at the cross (see Isaiah 53:4–5). You conquered death, hell, and the grave, and You rose again, so that we might share in Your life.

We confess, Lord, that we need You. We bring before You every place in our lives and marriage where we are weak, divided, hurting, or

burdened. We ask for Your forgiveness for where we have spoken in anger, withheld love, carried resentment, or failed to honor one another. Wash us clean, Jesus—in Your mercy, cover us with Your righteousness.

As we eat this bread, we receive Your healing. Heal our hearts where they are wounded. Heal our minds where they are anxious or tormented. Heal our bodies where they are sick or weak. Heal our marriage where it has been strained or broken. Let the same power that raised You from the dead now flow through us. Jesus, You stood in our place, bore our burdens, and overcame every trial. You are our source of strength, our anchor, and our help. As we eat this bread, we remember Your body—given so we could stand unshaken.

(Eat the bread)

As we drink this cup, we renew our covenant with You and with each other. We declare that we are Yours, and You are ours. We belong to You—as individuals and as a couple. Strengthen the bond between us. Let our love be patient, kind, humble, and enduring. Let forgiveness flow freely in our home. Let Your peace reign over our household. Jesus, thank You for Your blood, poured out for forgiveness and new life. As we drink this cup, we receive Your blood—poured out so we could walk in victory.

(Drink the cup)

Jesus, fill us with Your Spirit. Unite us in Your love. Draw us deeper into the mystery of union with You—that we may be one as You and

the Father are one. Teach us to love one another with Your supernatural love. Teach us to walk in Your ways. Teach us to see our marriage not only as partnership, but as a holy vessel that carries Your glory into this world.

We receive now—with faith and joy—the blessings You have promised. Blessings of peace, healing, provision, restoration, protection, wisdom, and overflowing grace. We stand in agreement, as one, declaring that no weapon formed against us shall prosper. We break every assignment of the enemy against our lives and marriage. We release blessing over our future, over our family, and over the generations to come.

We bring You our struggles, our weaknesses, and our fears. Strengthen us, Lord. Make us resilient—not by might, but by Your Spirit. Teach us to stand together in Your love.

Thank You, Jesus. Amen.

FINAL WORD

Resilience is not about never bending—it's about bending without breaking because your roots run deep in God. Let this week be a time of remembering how far He's brought you and how faithfully He holds you now.

COUPLES ACTIVITY: "OUR RESILIENCE STORY"

Set aside 30 minutes this week to reflect together:

- ی What has been one of the hardest seasons we've walked through?
- ی How did we grow stronger through it?
- ی How did we see God's hand at work?

Pray together: *"Lord, thank You for carrying us. Keep making us strong—in You, in love, and in faith. Amen."*

COUPLES ACTIVITY: "REMEMBER, RECOUNT, RENEW"

This week, mark the milestone of Week 40 by intentionally reflecting on your journey together—both over these devotional weeks and over your marriage as a whole.

STEP 1: REMEMBER

Find a quiet time together. Light a candle or sit somewhere peaceful.

Ask each other:

- ﺱ What are three challenges we've overcome together?
- ﺱ What are three ways we've seen God's faithfulness in our relationship?
- ﺱ What are three qualities we admire in each other that have grown over time?

STEP 2: RECOUNT

Take turns telling short "mini-stories" from your marriage—moments where you felt God's presence, where you laughed in hard times, where you came through something you thought might break you.

This is not about fixing anything—it's about recounting God's goodness and your shared resilience.

STEP 3: RENEW

Hold hands and pray something like: *"Lord, thank You for carrying us through every season—the easy ones and the hard ones. Thank You for the gift of 40 weeks of walking deeper in love and faith together. We ask You to renew us for the road ahead—fill us with fresh strength, fresh hope, and fresh joy. Help us to keep holding onto You and onto each other, one day at a time. Amen."*

Then, do one small, symbolic act:

- Write a short note to each other.
- Share a toast or special meal.
- Go for a walk and thank God aloud.
- Sit in silence and simply be together.

SPIRITUAL SIGNIFICANCE OF THE NUMBER 40 (BIBLICAL PERSPECTIVE)

The number 40 carries profound biblical meaning, often symbolizing testing, preparation, transition, and new beginnings.

Here are some key examples:

- **Noah:** It rained 40 days and 40 nights (see Genesis 7:12)—a period of judgment but also of cleansing, leading to a new world.

- **Moses:** He spent 40 days and nights on Mount Sinai (see Exodus 24:18)—receiving the Law and experiencing God's glory.

- **Israel:** The Israelites wandered 40 years in the wilderness (see Numbers 14:33-34)—a time of testing, purification, and preparation before entering the Promised Land.

- **Elijah:** He journeyed 40 days and nights to Mount Horeb (see 1 Kings 19:8)—moving from despair to a personal encounter with God.

- **Jesus:** He fasted 40 days in the wilderness (see Matthew 4:2)—preparing for His public ministry, enduring testing, and overcoming the enemy.

MEANING FOR YOUR MARRIAGE

Hitting Week 40 is spiritually significant:

- **It marks a season of completion and preparation**—a time to pause, reflect, and recognize that God has been preparing you for deeper growth.

- **It represents a transition from surviving to thriving**—not just enduring hard seasons but stepping into a place of renewal and new life.

- **It invites you to see your journey as sacred**—all the tests, the waiting, the refining moments have been forming something beautiful in your love, your character, and your faith.

So, this week is a spiritual marker in your marriage:

- ی A time to give thanks for what's behind,
- ی To trust God for what's ahead,
- ی And to remember that you are stepping into something new, together.

WEEK 40 MILESTONE

A SACRED PAUSE

A WORD OF CELEBRATION

You've arrived at Week 40—a sacred number in scripture, symbolizing testing, preparation, perseverance, and transition into new beginnings.

Throughout this devotional, you have walked together through themes of love, forgiveness, joy, prayer, healing, and resilience.

This moment is not about perfection or having "arrived." It's about marking the faithfulness of God and the faithfulness of your love—through the easy weeks and the hard weeks, through the moments you showed up tired, hopeful, or broken, and still chose to walk forward, together.

This is holy ground.

A REFLECTION ON THE NUMBER 40

In scripture, 40 is never random.

It's the number of God's refining work —

- 40 days of rain for Noah,
- 40 years of wilderness for Israel
- 40 days of fasting for Jesus

It's a number that signals: *Something is being made new.*

In your marriage, these 40 weeks symbolize:

- The burdens you've carried.
- The lessons you've learned.
- The love you've protected.

And the God who has walked with you every step of the way.

MILESTONE PRAYER BLESSING

"Lord, we stand at this milestone moment and give You thanks. Thank You for bringing us through 40 weeks of seeking You together. Thank You for the times we laughed, the times we cried, the times we failed, and the times we held on. Thank You for the grace that carried us and the love that anchored us. As we stand here, we ask: do a new thing in us. Renew our strength, deepen our joy, heal any place still hurting, and lift us into a new season of intimacy, faith, and purpose. We surrender our past, present, and future into Your hands, and we

declare that this marriage is Yours—for Your glory, Your story, and Your love to shine through. In Jesus' name. Amen."

A SYMBOLIC ACTION

Consider doing one symbolic act this week to mark the milestone:

- Write love letters or short blessings to each other.
- Light a candle together and pray.
- Go on a walk, thanking God aloud.
- Take communion with intentional gratitude.
- Place a small stone or token somewhere in your home as a "remembrance marker" of God's faithfulness.

FINAL ENCOURAGEMENT

This is not the end—this is the beginning of what's next.

You are stepping forward, not as the same people who began this journey, but as refined, strengthened, and blessed partners, anchored in a love that has been tested and sustained by God.

Breathe it in.
Bless it.
Celebrate it.

And keep walking, hand in hand, into all He has for you.

MYSTICAL UNION

(walking in the Spirit, authority, desire, legacy, union with Christ)

WEEK 41
PRACTICING HOSPITALITY—MAKING YOUR MARRIAGE A PLACE OF WELCOME

MEDITATION SCRIPTURES

"Offer hospitality to one another without grumbling. Each of you should use whatever gift you have received to serve others, as faithful stewards of God's grace."—1 Peter 4:9–10 (NIV)

"Do not forget to entertain strangers, for by so doing some people have entertained angels without knowing it."—Hebrews 13:2 (NKJV)

"Share with the Lord's people who are in need. Practice hospitality."—Romans 12:13 (NIV)

GUIDED MEDITATION ON SCRIPTURE

Sit together in a quiet moment.

Read the scriptures aloud slowly. Let the words *offer hospitality… serve others… entertain angels… practice hospitality* stir something in your hearts.

Reflect silently:

- ی How can we open our home, time, or table to others, even in small, simple ways?
- ی Where might God be inviting us to extend kindness, encouragement, or generosity?
- ی How does our marriage reflect the welcoming heart of Christ?

Sit quietly, asking God to bring one or two people or needs to mind this week.

QUOTE FOR TODAY

"The guest is a messenger of God, who comes in and leaves a blessing behind."

—*St. Benedict of Nursia*

WORD FOR THE WEEK

Hospitality is more than entertaining—it's a spiritual practice of welcome, presence, and love. When couples practice hospitality, they create not just a beautiful home, but a beautiful witness: a marriage that overflows to bless others.

In scripture, hospitality is deeply connected to God's heart—He welcomes the stranger, feeds the hungry, clothes the poor, and makes room for the lonely. When you open your home and your lives, even in small ways, you become living signs of His generous, welcoming love.

Hospitality doesn't have to be fancy. It can be sharing a meal, inviting someone for coffee, offering a listening ear, or simply making space for others to feel seen and loved. As a couple, it can also mean looking outward together: noticing needs in your church, neighborhood, or family, and offering what you have with joy.

This week, ask God to help you see your marriage as a vessel of hospitality. Let it become a place where others encounter grace, laughter, prayer, and hope, not because you are perfect, but because you are willing to share His love.

PSALM TO MEDITATE ON

"You prepare a table before me in the presence of my enemies; You anoint my head with oil; my cup overflows."—Psalm 23:5 (NKJV)

GUIDED MEDITATION ON THE PSALM

Read Psalm 23:5 slowly, focusing on the image of God preparing a table and your cup overflowing.

Ask together:

- Lord, where is our "cup" overflowing—where can we share from our blessings?
- Who might You be calling us to serve, encourage, or invite in this season?

Picture your marriage as a table set by God, with room for others to come and receive His goodness.

DECLARATIONS FOR THE WEEK

We declare:

- ⸲ Our home and marriage are places of welcome, grace, and love.
- ⸲ We offer hospitality with joy and generosity.
- ⸲ We share what we have, trusting God to multiply it.
- ⸲ We are faithful stewards of God's blessings.
- ⸲ Our hospitality reflects the heart of Jesus.

COMMUNION PRAYER

(Prepare bread (or a cracker) and a small cup of juice. Together, hold the bread and pray).

Lord Jesus Christ, we come before You now, humbled and grateful. You are the Bread of Life, the true Manna from heaven. You gave Your body to be broken for us, that we might be made whole—spirit, soul, and body. You poured out Your blood as the cup of the new covenant, that we might be cleansed, forgiven, and reconciled to God.

We pause to remember Your sacrifice. We remember Your wounds, Your love, Your victory. We remember that You carried our sickness, our grief, our sins, and our shame upon Yourself at the cross (see Isaiah 53:4–5). You conquered death, hell, and the grave, and You rose again, so that we might share in Your life.

We confess, Lord, that we need You. We bring before You every place in our lives and marriage where we are weak, divided, hurting, or

burdened. We ask for Your forgiveness for where we have spoken in anger, withheld love, carried resentment, or failed to honor one another. Wash us clean, Jesus—in Your mercy, cover us with Your righteousness.

As we eat this bread, we receive Your healing. Heal our hearts where they are wounded. Heal our minds where they are anxious or tormented. Heal our bodies where they are sick or weak. Heal our marriage where it has been strained or broken. Let the same power that raised You from the dead now flow through us. Jesus, You welcomed us when we were strangers. You opened Your arms, Your table, and Your heart to make us family. As we eat this bread, we remember Your body—broken to invite us in.

(Eat the bread)

As we drink this cup, we renew our covenant with You and with each other. We declare that we are Yours, and You are ours. We belong to You—as individuals and as a couple. Strengthen the bond between us. Let our love be patient, kind, humble, and enduring. Let forgiveness flow freely in our home. Let Your peace reign over our household. Jesus, thank You for Your blood, poured out for forgiveness and new life. As we drink this cup, we receive Your blood—poured out to make us one with You and with each other.

(Drink the cup)

Jesus, fill us with Your Spirit. Unite us in Your love. Draw us deeper into the mystery of union with You—that we may be one as You and

316

the Father are one. Teach us to love one another with Your supernatural love. Teach us to walk in Your ways. Teach us to see our marriage not only as partnership, but as a holy vessel that carries Your glory into this world.

We receive now—with faith and joy—the blessings You have promised. Blessings of peace, healing, provision, restoration, protection, wisdom, and overflowing grace. We stand in agreement, as one, declaring that no weapon formed against us shall prosper. We break every assignment of the enemy against our lives and marriage. We release blessing over our future, over our family, and over the generations to come.

Teach us to open our home, our time, and our lives. Help us love others as You have loved us. Let our marriage be a reflection of Your generous, welcoming heart.

Thank You, Jesus. Amen.

FINAL WORD

Hospitality is not about having a perfect home—it's about offering a welcoming heart. Let this week be a time to notice someone who needs a little space to breathe, to belong, to be blessed—and let God use you to offer it.

COUPLES ACTIVITY: "HOSPITALITY TOGETHER"

Set aside time this week to ask each other:

- ﺱ Who is one person or family we could invite, encourage, or bless?
- ﺱ What simple way can we open our home or hearts—a meal, a visit, a small gift, a prayer?

Make a plan together, pray over it, and do it joyfully—knowing that in loving others, you are honoring God.

WEEK 42
LIVING GENEROUSLY—GIVING FREELY, LOVING ABUNDANTLY

MEDITATION SCRIPTURES

"A generous person will prosper; whoever refreshes others will be refreshed."—Proverbs 11:25 (NIV)

"Remember this: Whoever sows sparingly will also reap sparingly, and whoever sows generously will also reap generously."—2 Corinthians 9:6 (NIV)

"Freely you have received; freely give."—Matthew 10:8 (NIV)

GUIDED MEDITATION ON SCRIPTURE

Sit together quietly, maybe after dinner or during a calm evening moment.

Read the scriptures aloud slowly. Let the words *generous... refresh... sow generously... freely give* stir your hearts.

Reflect silently:

- Where in our lives are we already practicing generosity— with each other, with others, with God?

ع Where might God be inviting us to open our hands and give more freely—whether of time, kindness, forgiveness, resources, or love?

ع How can we encourage each other to be joyful, generous givers?

Sit for a moment, imagining God filling your hands with blessings, not just for you, but to flow through you to others.

QUOTE FOR TODAY

"You possess only what you give; all the rest will be lost."
—*St. Catherine of Siena*

WORD FOR THE WEEK

Generosity is a lifestyle, not just an action. It's a posture of the heart that says, *"What I have—love, time, forgiveness, resources, wisdom—is a gift from God, meant to be shared."* In marriage, generosity means giving to each other, not out of duty, but out of joy. And as a couple, it means looking outward: *Who can we bless together?*

Many couples wait to be generous until they feel they "have enough"—enough money, time, energy, or emotional margin. But the kingdom of God works upside-down: when we pour out, God pours in. When we refresh others, we ourselves are refreshed. Generosity multiplies love, joy, and blessing in unexpected ways.

Generosity can be as simple as a kind word when you're tired, an unexpected note of encouragement, a decision to forgive quickly, or an invitation to someone in need. It's less about how much you give and more about how open your heart is.

This week, invite God to awaken a spirit of generosity in your marriage, not just to meet needs, but to reflect His generous love to each other and to the world.

PSALM TO MEDITATE ON

"You open Your hand and satisfy the desire of every living thing."—Psalm 145:16 (NKJV)

GUIDED MEDITATION ON THE PSALM

Read Psalm 145:16 slowly.

Ask together:

- Lord, where are You opening Your hand in our lives right now?
- How can we open our hands to reflect Your generosity— to each other and to those around us?

Picture God's open hand over your marriage, overflowing with grace, and your hands open beneath His, ready to give.

DECLARATIONS FOR THE WEEK

We declare:

- Our marriage is marked by generosity, not scarcity.
- We give freely because we have freely received.
- We refresh others and are refreshed in return.
- We are generous in love, forgiveness, time, and resources.
- God's blessings flow through us to bless the world.

COMMUNION PRAYER

(Prepare bread (or a cracker) and a small cup of juice. Together, hold the bread and pray).

Lord Jesus Christ, we come before You now, humbled and grateful. You are the Bread of Life, the true Manna from heaven. You gave Your body to be broken for us, that we might be made whole—spirit, soul, and body. You poured out Your blood as the cup of the new covenant, that we might be cleansed, forgiven, and reconciled to God.

We pause to remember Your sacrifice. We remember Your wounds, Your love, Your victory. We remember that You carried our sickness, our grief, our sins, and our shame upon Yourself at the cross (see Isaiah 53:4–5). You conquered death, hell, and the grave, and You rose again, so that we might share in Your life.

We confess, Lord, that we need You. We bring before You every place in our lives and marriage where we are weak, divided, hurting, or burdened. We ask for Your forgiveness for where we have spoken in

anger, withheld love, carried resentment, or failed to honor one another. Wash us clean, Jesus—in Your mercy, cover us with Your righteousness.

As we eat this bread, we receive Your healing. Heal our hearts where they are wounded. Heal our minds where they are anxious or tormented. Heal our bodies where they are sick or weak. Heal our marriage where it has been strained or broken. Let the same power that raised You from the dead now flow through us. Jesus, You gave everything for us—Your love, Your life, Your grace, Your Spirit. You held nothing back. As we eat this bread, we remember Your body— broken to make us whole.

(Eat the bread)

As we drink this cup, we renew our covenant with You and with each other. We declare that we are Yours, and You are ours. We belong to You—as individuals and as a couple. Strengthen the bond between us. Let our love be patient, kind, humble, and enduring. Let forgiveness flow freely in our home. Let Your peace reign over our household. Jesus, thank You for Your blood, poured out for forgiveness and new life. As we drink this cup, we receive Your blood—poured out so we might live abundantly.

(Drink the cup)

Jesus, fill us with Your Spirit. Unite us in Your love. Draw us deeper into the mystery of union with You—that we may be one as You and the Father are one. Teach us to love one another with Your

supernatural love. Teach us to walk in Your ways. Teach us to see our marriage not only as partnership, but as a holy vessel that carries Your glory into this world.

We receive now—with faith and joy—the blessings You have promised. Blessings of peace, healing, provision, restoration, protection, wisdom, and overflowing grace. We stand in agreement, as one, declaring that no weapon formed against us shall prosper. We break every assignment of the enemy against our lives and marriage. We release blessing over our future, over our family, and over the generations to come.

Make us generous, Lord—not only with our resources but with our hearts. Help us give as You give, love as You love, and pour out as You pour into us.

Thank You, Jesus. Amen.

FINAL WORD

Generosity is not something you wait to have—it's something you choose to live. Let this week be marked by small, joyful acts of giving that remind you both of how richly God has blessed you.

COUPLES ACTIVITY: "GENEROSITY CHALLENGE"

Together, choose one way to practice generosity this week:

ى Write encouraging notes to each other.

ے Help someone in need (financially, practically, or emotionally).

ے Volunteer together or give to a ministry.

ے Surprise someone with a small, meaningful gift.

At the end of the week, reflect: *"How did it feel to give? How did God meet us in it?"*

Then pray: *"Lord, make us a generous couple, overflowing with Your love."*

WEEK 43
LETTING GO OF CONTROL—TRUSTING GOD TOGETHER

MEDITATION SCRIPTURES

"Trust in the Lord with all your heart, and lean not on your own understanding; in all your ways submit to Him, and He will make your paths straight."—Proverbs 3:5–6 (NIV)

"Be still, and know that I am God."—Psalm 46:10 (NKJV)

"Cast your cares on the Lord and He will sustain you; He will never let the righteous be shaken."—Psalm 55:22 (NIV)

GUIDED MEDITATION ON SCRIPTURE

Sit together in a moment of quiet, maybe holding hands or resting close.

Read the scriptures aloud slowly. Let the words *trust... lean not... be still... cast your cares* wash over you.

Reflect silently:

- ◡ Where are we clinging to control—over finances, family decisions, work, health, or future plans?

ی What fears or anxieties are we carrying that God is inviting us to release?

ی How might we surrender more as a couple, trusting God's wisdom, timing, and love?

Sit for a moment in stillness, imagining yourselves gently placing your burdens into God's strong, faithful hands.

QUOTE FOR TODAY

"O Lord, You know what is best; let this or that be done, as You please. Give what You will, how much You will, and when You will. Do with me as You know best, as shall most please You, and be for Your greater honor."

—*Thomas à Kempis*

WORD FOR THE WEEK

Control is a tempting but heavy burden—and in marriage, it can show up in subtle or loud ways: trying to manage outcomes, fix problems, avoid vulnerability, or shape each other's growth. But control often leads to anxiety, frustration, or disappointment because we are trying to carry what only God can hold.

True freedom comes when we release control, not with passivity or neglect, but with trust. Trust that God sees what we cannot, loves more than we do, and is working even when we don't understand. When couples practice surrender together, they create space for peace, faith, and unity to grow.

Letting go may look like praying over financial fears, blessing each other's dreams without forcing them, releasing perfectionism, or saying, *"God, we trust You with this."* It's less about giving up, and more about handing over, day by day.

This week, notice where you're gripping too tightly—and gently practice letting go. Ask God to help you trust Him together—as individuals and as one heart.

PSALM TO MEDITATE ON

"Commit your way to the Lord; trust in Him and He will do this."—Psalm 37:5 (NIV)

GUIDED MEDITATION ON THE PSALM

Read Psalm 37:5 slowly.

Ask together:

- ی Lord, what are You inviting us to commit into Your hands this week?
- ی Where do we need to loosen our grip and let You lead?

Picture yourselves standing together before God, opening your hands, releasing whatever you've been carrying.

DECLARATIONS FOR THE WEEK

We declare:

- ى We trust God more than we trust our own plans.
- ى We release the need to control and receive God's peace.
- ى We surrender our marriage, our future, and our burdens to God.
- ى God is faithful, wise, and loving in every detail.
- ى We walk forward together in freedom and trust.

COMMUNION PRAYER

(Prepare bread (or a cracker) and a small cup of juice. Together, hold the bread and pray).

Lord Jesus Christ, we come before You now, humbled and grateful. You are the Bread of Life, the true Manna from heaven. You gave Your body to be broken for us, that we might be made whole—spirit, soul, and body. You poured out Your blood as the cup of the new covenant, that we might be cleansed, forgiven, and reconciled to God.

We pause to remember Your sacrifice. We remember Your wounds, Your love, Your victory. We remember that You carried our sickness, our grief, our sins, and our shame upon Yourself at the cross (see Isaiah 53:4–5). You conquered death, hell, and the grave, and You rose again, so that we might share in Your life.

We confess, Lord, that we need You. We bring before You every place in our lives and marriage where we are weak, divided, hurting, or

burdened. We ask for Your forgiveness for where we have spoken in anger, withheld love, carried resentment, or failed to honor one another. Wash us clean, Jesus—in Your mercy, cover us with Your righteousness.

As we eat this bread, we receive Your healing. Heal our hearts where they are wounded. Heal our minds where they are anxious or tormented. Heal our bodies where they are sick or weak. Heal our marriage where it has been strained or broken. Let the same power that raised You from the dead now flow through us. Jesus, You surrendered completely to the Father's will—not out of defeat, but out of love and trust. You laid down Your life to bring us into peace. As we eat this bread, we remember Your body—given freely.

(Eat the bread)

As we drink this cup, we renew our covenant with You and with each other. We declare that we are Yours, and You are ours. We belong to You—as individuals and as a couple. Strengthen the bond between us. Let our love be patient, kind, humble, and enduring. Let forgiveness flow freely in our home. Let Your peace reign over our household. Jesus, thank You for Your blood, poured out for forgiveness and new life. As we drink this cup, we receive Your blood—poured out in perfect surrender.

(Drink the cup)

Jesus, fill us with Your Spirit. Unite us in Your love. Draw us deeper into the mystery of union with You—that we may be one as You and

the Father are one. Teach us to love one another with Your supernatural love. Teach us to walk in Your ways. Teach us to see our marriage not only as partnership, but as a holy vessel that carries Your glory into this world.

We receive now—with faith and joy—the blessings You have promised. Blessings of peace, healing, provision, restoration, protection, wisdom, and overflowing grace. We stand in agreement, as one, declaring that no weapon formed against us shall prosper. We break every assignment of the enemy against our lives and marriage. We release blessing over our future, over our family, and over the generations to come.

Teach us to let go of control, Lord. Help us trust You with our lives, our marriage, and our future. Lead us into the rest and peace that come from surrender.

Thank You, Jesus. Amen.

FINAL WORD

Letting go is not weakness—it's strength in the Spirit. This week, open your hands, release your burdens, and walk together in the freedom of trusting God.

COUPLES ACTIVITY: "THE LET-GO PRAYER"

Set aside a quiet time together. Each of you share:

- ی One area where you feel tempted to control or carry too much.

- ی One fear or burden you want to entrust to God.

Write these down or speak them aloud. Then pray together: *"Lord, we release these into Your hands. Teach us to trust, to rest, and to follow You, not in fear, but in faith. Amen."*

WEEK 44
WALKING IN SPIRITUAL AUTHORITY— STANDING STRONG IN FAITH TOGETHER

MEDITATION SCRIPTURES

"I have given you authority... to overcome all the power of the enemy; nothing will harm you."—Luke 10:19 (NIV)

"Submit yourselves, then, to God. Resist the devil, and he will flee from you."—James 4:7 (NIV)

"For the weapons of our warfare are not carnal but mighty in God for pulling down strongholds."—2 Corinthians 10:4 (NKJV)

GUIDED MEDITATION ON SCRIPTURE

Sit quietly together, maybe with hands joined or in a posture of strength.

Read the scriptures aloud slowly. Let the words *authority... overcome... resist... weapons mighty in God* stir your hearts with courage and faith.

Reflect silently:

- ی Where in our marriage or home do we need to stand stronger spiritually?
- ی What battles or struggles are we facing that need prayer, not just human effort?
- ی How can we agree together to stand in the authority God has given us?

Take a deep breath, picturing yourselves clothed in God's strength, not just your own.

QUOTE FOR TODAY

"The soul that walks in love walks in power, for perfect love casts out fear and strengthens the spirit."

—*Teresa of Ávila*

WORD FOR THE WEEK

As a couple, you are not powerless. You are not at the mercy of circumstances, attacks, or fears. In Christ, you have been given authority—authority to pray, to stand, to resist darkness, and to release God's peace and love into your home.

Spiritual authority is not about shouting or striving—it's about knowing who you are in Christ and standing firm. It's about resisting lies with truth, pushing back fear with faith, and covering your marriage, family, and home with prayer and blessing. Together, you are stronger. Together, your prayers shake things in the unseen realm.

There will be times when you sense heaviness, tension, discouragement, or attack—these are not just natural challenges but spiritual moments calling you to rise in prayer. Jesus has already overcome, and He invites you to stand in His victory, together.

This week, pray boldly as a couple. Declare God's promises over your home. Push back anything that does not reflect His peace, love, and truth. Walk in the authority He has given you, not in fear, but in confidence.

PSALM TO MEDITATE ON

"The Lord is my light and my salvation; whom shall I fear? The Lord is the strength of my life; of whom shall I be afraid?"—Psalm 27:1 (NKJV)

GUIDED MEDITATION ON THE PSALM

Read Psalm 27:1 aloud slowly.

Ask together:

- ى Lord, where are we feeling afraid or under pressure?
- ى How can we stand in Your strength and authority this week?

Picture God as your light, your defender, and your stronghold—surrounding your marriage with His presence.

DECLARATIONS FOR THE WEEK

We declare:

- ☞ We are covered by the blood of Jesus and stand in His victory.
- ☞ We resist fear, discouragement, and every lie of the enemy.
- ☞ We release peace, love, and truth over our home.
- ☞ We stand together in prayer, faith, and spiritual authority.
- ☞ No weapon formed against us will prosper.

COMMUNION PRAYER

(Prepare bread (or a cracker) and a small cup of juice. Together, hold the bread and pray).

Lord Jesus Christ, we come before You now, humbled and grateful. You are the Bread of Life, the true Manna from heaven. You gave Your body to be broken for us, that we might be made whole—spirit, soul, and body. You poured out Your blood as the cup of the new covenant, that we might be cleansed, forgiven, and reconciled to God.

We pause to remember Your sacrifice. We remember Your wounds, Your love, Your victory. We remember that You carried our sickness, our grief, our sins, and our shame upon Yourself at the cross (see Isaiah 53:4–5). You conquered death, hell, and the grave, and You rose again, so that we might share in Your life.

We confess, Lord, that we need You. We bring before You every place in our lives and marriage where we are weak, divided, hurting, or

336

burdened. We ask for Your forgiveness for where we have spoken in anger, withheld love, carried resentment, or failed to honor one another. Wash us clean, Jesus—in Your mercy, cover us with Your righteousness.

As we eat this bread, we receive Your healing. Heal our hearts where they are wounded. Heal our minds where they are anxious or tormented. Heal our bodies where they are sick or weak. Heal our marriage where it has been strained or broken. Let the same power that raised You from the dead now flow through us. Jesus, You are our Savior, our Champion, and our King. By Your cross, You defeated sin, death, and darkness. In You, we stand free and victorious. As we eat this bread, we remember Your body—broken to break every chain.

(Eat the bread)

As we drink this cup, we renew our covenant with You and with each other. We declare that we are Yours, and You are ours. We belong to You—as individuals and as a couple. Strengthen the bond between us. Let our love be patient, kind, humble, and enduring. Let forgiveness flow freely in our home. Let Your peace reign over our household. Jesus, thank You for Your blood, poured out for forgiveness and new life. As we drink this cup, we receive Your blood—covering us with life, love, and power.

(Drink the cup)

Jesus, fill us with Your Spirit. Unite us in Your love. Draw us deeper into the mystery of union with You—that we may be one as You and

the Father are one. Teach us to love one another with Your supernatural love. Teach us to walk in Your ways. Teach us to see our marriage not only as partnership, but as a holy vessel that carries Your glory into this world.

We receive now—with faith and joy—the blessings You have promised. Blessings of peace, healing, provision, restoration, protection, wisdom, and overflowing grace. We stand in agreement, as one, declaring that no weapon formed against us shall prosper. We break every assignment of the enemy against our lives and marriage. We release blessing over our future, over our family, and over the generations to come.

We claim Your peace, Your authority, and Your victory over our marriage and home. Strengthen us to stand, pray, and love boldly.

Thank You, Jesus. Amen.

FINAL WORD

You are not powerless. You are beloved and empowered in Christ. This week, stand together, not just as husband and wife, but as a spiritual team, clothed in God's strength and armed with His promises.

COUPLES ACTIVITY: "OUR SPIRITUAL STAND"

Set aside time this week to pray boldly together:

- ﺱ Name one or two areas where you need God's breakthrough.

ی Declare aloud God's promises over those areas (look up scriptures if needed).

Pray a blessing over each other: *"In Jesus' name, I bless you with strength, peace, and joy."*

End by thanking God: *"Lord, thank You that we are not alone—we stand in Your love and Your victory. Amen."*

SPIRITUAL WARFARE PRAYER FOR OUR MARRIAGE

Heavenly Father,

We come before You together as one, united in Christ, covered by His blood, and filled with His Spirit. Thank You that You are our refuge, our strength, and our victory. Thank You that no weapon formed against us will prosper and that greater is He who is in us than he who is in the world.

In the name of Jesus, we take authority over every scheme, lie, or attack of the enemy against our marriage, our home, our minds, our bodies, and our relationship. We break the power of fear, division, discouragement, resentment, and confusion. We declare that they have no place here. We resist the devil, and we thank You, God, that when we do, he must flee.

Lord, clothe us with the armor of God:

- ﺱ the belt of truth
- ﺱ the breastplate of righteousness
- ﺱ the shoes of the gospel of peace
- ﺱ the shield of faith
- ﺱ the helmet of salvation
- ﺱ and the sword of the Spirit, which is Your Word.

Teach us to stand firm together—to pray together, to forgive quickly, to speak life, to show grace, and to cover our home in Your peace.

We invite You, Holy Spirit, to fill every room, every conversation, every thought, and every decision.

Let Your presence be the atmosphere of our home.
Let Your love drive out all fear.
Let Your light push out all darkness.
Let Your truth silence every lie.

We bless each other now:

- I bless my spouse with strength, peace, health, and joy.
- I bless our marriage to be a testimony of Your faithfulness and love.
- I bless our home to be a place of safety, laughter, healing, and Your glory.

Thank You, Jesus, that You fight for us, go before us, and hold us together.

We rest in You, we stand in You, and we walk forward in victory—together.

In Jesus' mighty name we pray. Amen.

WEEK 45
PERSEVERING IN FAITH—HOLDING ON, HAND IN HAND

MEDITATION SCRIPTURES

"Let us hold fast the confession of our hope without wavering, for He who promised is faithful."—Hebrews 10:23 (NKJV)

"Consider it pure joy, my brothers and sisters, whenever you face trials of many kinds, because you know that the testing of your faith produces perseverance."—James 1:2–3 (NIV)

"We do not lose heart. Though outwardly we are wasting away, yet inwardly we are being renewed day by day."—2 Corinthians 4:16 (NIV)

GUIDED MEDITATION ON SCRIPTURE

Sit quietly together, maybe holding hands or resting close.

Read the scriptures aloud slowly. Let the words *hold fast... hope without wavering... testing produces perseverance... do not lose heart* settle deeply.

Reflect silently:

- و Where are we being called to persevere—in our marriage, family, health, dreams, finances, or faith?
- و What has God already carried us through, and how has our faith grown?
- و Where do we need to encourage each other to keep trusting, even when we don't yet see answers?

Picture God strengthening your hands as you hold each other's.

QUOTE FOR TODAY

"He who has God finds the long road short, and the bitter road sweet."

—*Thomas à Kempis*

WORD FOR THE WEEK

Faith is easy when everything goes smoothly, but it becomes real, strong, and beautiful when tested. In marriage, perseverance in faith means choosing hope together, even when prayers take time, when challenges feel heavy, or when you're tempted to give up.

God never promised an easy path, but He promises His presence, His faithfulness, and His goodness in every season. As a couple, you are not just enduring; you are learning to lean on Him together, to pray through pain, to laugh in waiting, to worship in uncertainty, and to walk forward in hope.

Perseverance doesn't mean pretending you're fine. It means showing up for each other, reminding one another of God's promises, and holding on—hand in hand, heart to heart—until the breakthrough comes. It means saying, *"We will trust, we will love, we will hope— no matter what."*

This week, look back on what God has already done and look forward in hope. Encourage each other, pray together, and keep walking. You are not alone, and the One who promised is faithful.

PSALM TO MEDITATE ON

"Wait for the Lord; be strong and take heart and wait for the Lord."—Psalm 27:14 (NIV)

GUIDED MEDITATION ON THE PSALM

Read Psalm 27 slowly, letting the call to wait and be strong echo in your heart.

Ask together:

- ؈ Lord, what are You asking us to wait for with hope?
- ؈ Where do we need fresh strength to persevere this week?

Picture yourselves holding hands, with God standing beside you, whispering, *"I am with you."*

DECLARATIONS FOR THE WEEK

We declare:

- We will not give up—we will hold fast to God's promises.
- Our faith is being refined, strengthened, and made beautiful.
- We walk forward in trust, not fear; in hope, not despair.
- God is faithful, present, and working, even when we don't see it yet.
- Together, we will persevere, hand in hand, heart to heart.

COMMUNION PRAYER

(Prepare bread (or a cracker) and a small cup of juice. Together, hold the bread and pray).

Lord Jesus Christ, we come before You now, humbled and grateful. You are the Bread of Life, the true Manna from heaven. You gave Your body to be broken for us, that we might be made whole—spirit, soul, and body. You poured out Your blood as the cup of the new covenant, that we might be cleansed, forgiven, and reconciled to God.

We pause to remember Your sacrifice. We remember Your wounds, Your love, Your victory. We remember that You carried our sickness, our grief, our sins, and our shame upon Yourself at the cross (see Isaiah 53:4–5). You conquered death, hell, and the grave, and You rose again, so that we might share in Your life.

We confess, Lord, that we need You. We bring before You every place in our lives and marriage where we are weak, divided, hurting, or burdened. We ask for Your forgiveness for where we have spoken in anger, withheld love, carried resentment, or failed to honor one another. Wash us clean, Jesus—in Your mercy, cover us with Your righteousness.

As we eat this bread, we receive Your healing. Heal our hearts where they are wounded. Heal our minds where they are anxious or tormented. Heal our bodies where they are sick or weak. Heal our marriage where it has been strained or broken. Let the same power that raised You from the dead now flow through us. Jesus, You endured the cross for the joy set before You—and You are our joy, our hope, and our strength. As we eat this bread, we remember Your body—given to carry our burdens.

(Eat the bread)

As we drink this cup, we renew our covenant with You and with each other. We declare that we are Yours, and You are ours. We belong to You—as individuals and as a couple. Strengthen the bond between us. Let our love be patient, kind, humble, and enduring. Let forgiveness flow freely in our home. Let Your peace reign over our household. Jesus, thank You for Your blood, poured out for forgiveness and new life. As we drink this cup, we receive Your blood—poured out to give us life and hope.

(Drink the cup)

Jesus, fill us with Your Spirit. Unite us in Your love. Draw us deeper into the mystery of union with You—that we may be one as You and the Father are one. Teach us to love one another with Your supernatural love. Teach us to walk in Your ways. Teach us to see our marriage not only as partnership, but as a holy vessel that carries Your glory into this world.

We receive now—with faith and joy—the blessings You have promised. Blessings of peace, healing, provision, restoration, protection, wisdom, and overflowing grace. We stand in agreement, as one, declaring that no weapon formed against us shall prosper. We break every assignment of the enemy against our lives and marriage. We release blessing over our future, over our family, and over the generations to come.

Help us persevere, Lord. Strengthen our hearts, renew our faith, and remind us that we are not walking alone. Teach us to wait with joy, to trust with peace, and to hope with confidence.

Thank You, Jesus. Amen.

FINAL WORD

Perseverance is not about gritting your teeth—it's about holding onto God and each other with open, trusting hearts. Let this week be a time of quiet courage, deep encouragement, and renewed hope.

COUPLES ACTIVITY: "OUR FAITH STORY"

Set aside time this week to reflect and share:

- ی What is one challenge we've already seen God bring us through?
- ی What are we currently waiting on, hoping for, or trusting God with?
- ی How can we encourage each other to keep believing?

End by praying together: *"Lord, strengthen our faith, renew our hope, and carry us as we wait. Help us walk forward in love and trust, together. Amen."*

WEEK 46
RENEWING OUR MINDS—THINKING GOD'S WAY TOGETHER

MEDITATION SCRIPTURES

"Do not be conformed to this world, but be transformed by the renewing of your mind, that you may prove what is that good and acceptable and perfect will of God."—Romans 12:2 (NKJV)

"We take captive every thought to make it obedient to Christ." —2 Corinthians 10:5 (NIV)

"Finally, brothers and sisters, whatever is true, whatever is noble, whatever is right, whatever is pure, whatever is lovely, whatever is admirable—if anything is excellent or praiseworthy—think about such things."—Philippians 4:8 (NIV)

GUIDED MEDITATION ON SCRIPTURE

Sit together quietly, maybe with eyes closed or hands held.

Read the scriptures aloud slowly. Let the words *renewing... take captive... think about such things* settle over your hearts.

Reflect silently:

- ﺱ Where have negative or anxious thoughts been affecting us—personally or as a couple?
- ﺱ What thought patterns do we need to release and replace with God's truth?
- ﺱ How can we help each other guard our minds and focus on what is true and life-giving?

Imagine God's truth washing over your minds like fresh, living water.

QUOTE FOR TODAY

"The soul's health is found in turning its thoughts continually to God, until His truth becomes its home and His love its light."

—*Brother Lawrence*

WORD FOR THE WEEK

Our thoughts shape our emotions, our actions, and even the atmosphere of our marriage. What we dwell on—worries, comparisons, past wounds, or God's promises, love, and peace—determines the climate of our home and our hearts.

Renewing your minds together is a daily practice. It means noticing the lies or fears that creep in and replacing them with God's truth. It means speaking encouragement over each other, praying over anxious thoughts, and choosing to focus on gratitude, hope, and love.

The world bombards us with noise, negativity, and pressure. But as a couple, you can create a counterculture in your home—a place where God's Word is the standard, where truth is spoken with kindness, and where your minds are continually refreshed by His presence.

This week, be intentional about what you meditate on together. Catch yourselves when you fall into spirals of worry or complaint and gently help each other turn back toward what is true, noble, pure, and praiseworthy.

PSALM TO MEDITATE ON

"Search me, O God, and know my heart; test me and know my anxious thoughts. See if there is any offensive way in me, and lead me in the way everlasting."—Psalm 139:23–24 (NIV)

GUIDED MEDITATION ON THE PSALM

Read Psalm 139:23-24 slowly, almost like a whisper.

Ask together:

- ပ Lord, what anxious or harmful thoughts do we need to release this week?
- ပ How can we help each other stay rooted in Your truth and love?

Picture God gently clearing away anxious or false thoughts, and planting seeds of peace and renewal.

DECLARATIONS FOR THE WEEK

We declare:

- ও Our minds are being renewed by God's truth every day.
- ও We take captive negative, fearful, or harmful thoughts and replace them with God's promises.
- ও We help each other focus on what is good, true, lovely, and praiseworthy.
- ও God's truth shapes our words, our attitudes, and our marriage.
- ও We are being transformed into His likeness, together.

COMMUNION PRAYER

(Prepare bread (or a cracker) and a small cup of juice. Together, hold the bread and pray).

Lord Jesus Christ, we come before You now, humbled and grateful. You are the Bread of Life, the true Manna from heaven. You gave Your body to be broken for us, that we might be made whole—spirit, soul, and body. You poured out Your blood as the cup of the new covenant, that we might be cleansed, forgiven, and reconciled to God.

We pause to remember Your sacrifice. We remember Your wounds, Your love, Your victory. We remember that You carried our sickness, our grief, our sins, and our shame upon Yourself at the cross (see Isaiah 53:4–5). You conquered death, hell, and the grave, and You rose again, so that we might share in Your life.

We confess, Lord, that we need You. We bring before You every place in our lives and marriage where we are weak, divided, hurting, or burdened. We ask for Your forgiveness for where we have spoken in anger, withheld love, carried resentment, or failed to honor one another. Wash us clean, Jesus—in Your mercy, cover us with Your righteousness.

As we eat this bread, we receive Your healing. Heal our hearts where they are wounded. Heal our minds where they are anxious or tormented. Heal our bodies where they are sick or weak. Heal our marriage where it has been strained or broken. Let the same power that raised You from the dead now flow through us. Jesus, You are the Truth, the Way, and the Life. You have given us the mind of Christ—a mind filled with peace, love, and wisdom. As we eat this bread, we remember Your body—given to transform our whole being.

(Eat the bread)

As we drink this cup, we renew our covenant with You and with each other. We declare that we are Yours, and You are ours. We belong to You—as individuals and as a couple. Strengthen the bond between us. Let our love be patient, kind, humble, and enduring. Let forgiveness flow freely in our home. Let Your peace reign over our household. Jesus, thank You for Your blood, poured out for forgiveness and new life. As we drink this cup, we receive Your blood—poured out to renew and cleanse us.

(Drink the cup)

Jesus, fill us with Your Spirit. Unite us in Your love. Draw us deeper into the mystery of union with You—that we may be one as You and the Father are one. Teach us to love one another with Your supernatural love. Teach us to walk in Your ways. Teach us to see our marriage not only as partnership, but as a holy vessel that carries Your glory into this world.

We receive now—with faith and joy—the blessings You have promised. Blessings of peace, healing, provision, restoration, protection, wisdom, and overflowing grace. We stand in agreement, as one, declaring that no weapon formed against us shall prosper. We break every assignment of the enemy against our lives and marriage. We release blessings over our future, over our family, and over the generations to come.

Renew our minds, Lord. Heal our thoughts. Fill our hearts with Your perspective. Help us think, speak, and love like You—with grace and truth.

Thank You, Jesus. Amen.

FINAL WORD

You don't have to believe every thought you think. Let this week be a time of quietly and intentionally renewing your minds together—and watching how God's truth brings life, clarity, and peace.

COUPLES ACTIVITY: "THE THOUGHT CHECK-IN"

Set aside time this week to gently ask each other:

- ٯ What's been on your mind the most this week?
- ٯ Is there a thought that's been weighing you down or stealing peace?
- ٯ What is one truth from God's Word we can speak over that?

Pray together: *"Lord, help us to think Your thoughts, to speak Your truth, and to encourage each other toward peace and joy. Amen."*

WEEK 47
PRACTICING VULNERABILITY—THE COURAGE TO BE KNOWN

MEDITATION SCRIPTURES

"Therefore, confess your sins to each other and pray for each other so that you may be healed. The prayer of a righteous person is powerful and effective."—James 5:16 (NIV)

"Two are better than one... If either of them falls down, one can help the other up."—Ecclesiastes 4:9–10 (NIV)

"Carry each other's burdens, and in this way you will fulfill the law of Christ."—Galatians 6:2 (NIV)

GUIDED MEDITATION ON SCRIPTURE

Sit together quietly, perhaps in a safe, comfortable space.

Read the scriptures aloud slowly. Let the words *confess... pray for each other... help the other up... carry each other's burdens* settle into your heart.

Reflect silently:

- ﺱ Where have I been hesitant to share my true feelings, fears, or needs with my spouse?
- ﺱ How can we create more safety and grace in our relationship for honesty and vulnerability?
- ﺱ How can we carry each other's burdens without trying to fix, judge, or control?

Imagine God's gentle presence wrapping around you both, creating a space of safety and love.

QUOTE FOR TODAY

"The soul that hides nothing from God will find peace; the soul that hides nothing from its neighbor will find love."
—*Julian of Norwich*

WORD FOR THE WEEK

Vulnerability is the soil where true intimacy grows. It's the courageous act of letting yourself be seen—not just your strengths, but your fears, wounds, longings, and dreams. In marriage, vulnerability says: *"Here I am. Can you love me here too?"*

Many couples grow distant not because they stop loving each other, but because they stop sharing their inner lives. Walls go up; hearts shut down; the connection becomes shallow or functional. But God invites you into something deeper: to carry each other's burdens, to lift each other up, to pray and heal together.

Practicing vulnerability means creating a marriage where honesty is met with compassion, where confession leads to healing, and where weakness is not punished but held with tenderness. This doesn't mean oversharing or dumping everything at once—it means learning, little by little, to trust each other with your real selves.

This week, take a small step: share something real. It might be a small worry, a personal dream, a hidden hurt, or a deep longing. Listen well. Pray together. Let God deepen your bond through the sacred courage of being known.

PSALM TO MEDITATE ON

"Search me, God, and know my heart; test me and know my anxious thoughts. See if there is any offensive way in me, and lead me in the way everlasting."—Psalm 139:23–24 (NIV)

GUIDED MEDITATION ON THE PSALM

Read Psalm 139:23-24 slowly, letting it open your heart before God.

Ask together:

- ☙ Lord, what in my heart needs to be shared with You and with my spouse?
- ☙ Help us make space to listen, understand, and hold each other with grace.

Picture God standing with you both, helping you carry what's been hidden or heavy.

DECLARATIONS FOR THE WEEK

We declare:

- ِ We create a safe space for honesty and vulnerability.
- ِ We carry each other's burdens with love and grace.
- ِ We listen deeply, without judgment or fear.
- ِ Our marriage grows in intimacy, trust, and healing.
- ِ God meets us in our openness and knits our hearts together.

COMMUNION PRAYER

(Prepare bread (or a cracker) and a small cup of juice. Together, hold the bread and pray).

Lord Jesus Christ, we come before You now, humbled and grateful. You are the Bread of Life, the true Manna from heaven. You gave Your body to be broken for us, that we might be made whole—spirit, soul, and body. You poured out Your blood as the cup of the new covenant, that we might be cleansed, forgiven, and reconciled to God.

We pause to remember Your sacrifice. We remember Your wounds, Your love, Your victory. We remember that You carried our sickness, our grief, our sins, and our shame upon Yourself at the cross (see Isaiah 53:4–5). You conquered death, hell, and the grave, and You rose again, so that we might share in Your life.

We confess, Lord, that we need You. We bring before You every place in our lives and marriage where we are weak, divided, hurting, or

burdened. We ask for Your forgiveness for where we have spoken in anger, withheld love, carried resentment, or failed to honor one another. Wash us clean, Jesus—in Your mercy, cover us with Your righteousness.

As we eat this bread, we receive Your healing. Heal our hearts where they are wounded. Heal our minds where they are anxious or tormented. Heal our bodies where they are sick or weak. Heal our marriage where it has been strained or broken. Let the same power that raised You from the dead now flow through us. Jesus, You see us fully and love us completely. You are our safe place, our healer, and our friend. As we eat this bread, we remember Your body—broken so we might be made whole.

(Eat the bread)

As we drink this cup, we renew our covenant with You and with each other. We declare that we are Yours, and You are ours. We belong to You—as individuals and as a couple. Strengthen the bond between us. Let our love be patient, kind, humble, and enduring. Let forgiveness flow freely in our home. Let Your peace reign over our household. Jesus, thank You for Your blood, poured out for forgiveness and new life. As we drink this cup, we receive Your blood—poured out to cover us in love and grace.

(Drink the cup)

Jesus, fill us with Your Spirit. Unite us in Your love. Draw us deeper into the mystery of union with You—that we may be one as You and

the Father are one. Teach us to love one another with Your supernatural love. Teach us to walk in Your ways. Teach us to see our marriage not only as partnership, but as a holy vessel that carries Your glory into this world.

We receive now—with faith and joy—the blessings You have promised. Blessings of peace, healing, provision, restoration, protection, wisdom, and overflowing grace. We stand in agreement, as one, declaring that no weapon formed against us shall prosper. We break every assignment of the enemy against our lives and marriage. We release blessings over our future, over our family, and over the generations to come.

Teach us to be open, Lord—with You and with each other. Help us confess, forgive, listen, and heal. Make our marriage a place where Your love is felt deeply and shared freely.

Thank You, Jesus. Amen.

FINAL WORD

Vulnerability is not weakness—it's the doorway to deeper love. This week, take the small, brave step of opening your heart and holding your spouse's heart with tenderness.

COUPLES ACTIVITY: "THE HONEST MOMENT"

Set aside quiet time this week to ask each other:

- What's one thing you're carrying on your heart right now?

ﺱ What's one thing you need encouragement or prayer for?

ﺱ How can I hold that with you, without fixing or judging?

Pray together: *"Lord, help us carry each other's hearts well. Give us courage to share and compassion to listen. Make our marriage a place of deep love. Amen."*

WEEK 48
CELEBRATING VICTORIES—REJOICING IN WHAT GOD HAS DONE

MEDITATION SCRIPTURES

"Rejoice in the Lord always. Again I will say, rejoice!"—Philippians 4:4 (NKJV)

"The Lord has done great things for us, and we are filled with joy."—Psalm 126:3 (NIV)

"Give thanks to the Lord, for He is good; His love endures forever."—Psalm 136:1 (NIV)

GUIDED MEDITATION ON SCRIPTURE

Sit together quietly, maybe holding hands or lighting a candle.

Read the scriptures aloud slowly. Let the words *rejoice… great things… give thanks… His love endures* fill your hearts.

Reflect silently:

- ९ What victories—big or small—has God brought us through this year?
- ९ Where have we grown as individuals and as a couple?

ﺱ How can we pause to thank and celebrate God, instead of just rushing to the next thing?

Picture God smiling over you, delighting in your journey and the love you share.

QUOTE FOR TODAY

"Joy is the infallible sign of the presence of God."
—*Pierre Teilhard de Chardin*

WORD FOR THE WEEK

It's easy to rush through life, barely pausing to notice what God has done. You face a challenge, push through, move on. You pray for something, receive it, and soon turn to the next need. But God invites you to stop, notice, and celebrate—to mark the victories, give thanks, and rejoice together.

Celebrating victories as a couple deepens your gratitude, strengthens your bond, and reminds you that you are not doing life alone—you are walking with a faithful, generous God. Victory isn't only about big moments; it's also about small triumphs: a week of better communication, an answered prayer, a breakthrough in patience, a season of peace.

When you pause to celebrate, you shift the atmosphere of your home. You replace worry with worship, exhaustion with joy, and striving with gratitude. You honor what God has done and open your hearts to what He still wants to do.

This week, look back with thankful eyes. Name the victories, honor the progress, and rejoice together. Let your home echo with gratitude and joy.

PSALM TO MEDITATE ON

"You have turned my mourning into joyful dancing. You have taken away my clothes of mourning and clothed me with joy, that I might sing praises to You and not be silent."—Psalm 30:11–12 (NLT)

GUIDED MEDITATION ON THE PSALM

Read Psalm 30:11-12 slowly, feeling the joy in the words.

Ask together:

- Lord, what victories have You brought us through—even in hard seasons?
- How can we praise and thank You with full hearts this week?

Imagine yourself dancing lightly in God's presence, filled with gratitude.

DECLARATIONS FOR THE WEEK

We declare:

- We rejoice in the Lord always—in small things and big.
- We celebrate every victory God has given us.

- ى We are a couple marked by gratitude and joy.
- ى Our home is filled with praise and thanksgiving.
- ى God's goodness will carry us forward with hope.

COMMUNION PRAYER

**(Prepare bread (or a cracker) and a small cup of juice.
Together, hold the bread and pray).**

Lord Jesus Christ, we come before You now, humbled and grateful. You are the Bread of Life, the true Manna from heaven. You gave Your body to be broken for us, that we might be made whole—spirit, soul, and body. You poured out Your blood as the cup of the new covenant, that we might be cleansed, forgiven, and reconciled to God.

We pause to remember Your sacrifice. We remember Your wounds, Your love, Your victory. We remember that You carried our sickness, our grief, our sins, and our shame upon Yourself at the cross (see Isaiah 53:4–5). You conquered death, hell, and the grave, and You rose again, so that we might share in Your life.

We confess, Lord, that we need You. We bring before You every place in our lives and marriage where we are weak, divided, hurting, or burdened. We ask for Your forgiveness for where we have spoken in anger, withheld love, carried resentment, or failed to honor one another. Wash us clean, Jesus—in Your mercy, cover us with Your righteousness.

As we eat this bread, we receive Your healing. Heal our hearts where they are wounded. Heal our minds where they are anxious or

tormented. Heal our bodies where they are sick or weak. Heal our marriage where it has been strained or broken. Let the same power that raised You from the dead now flow through us. Jesus, You are our greatest victory—You have conquered sin, death, fear, and shame. In You, we walk in freedom, joy, and life. As we eat this bread, we remember Your body—broken so we might be whole.

(Eat the bread)

As we drink this cup, we renew our covenant with You and with each other. We declare that we are Yours, and You are ours. We belong to You—as individuals and as a couple. Strengthen the bond between us. Let our love be patient, kind, humble, and enduring. Let forgiveness flow freely in our home. Let Your peace reign over our household. Jesus, thank You for Your blood, poured out for forgiveness and new life. As we drink this cup, we receive Your blood—poured out so we might live victorious.

(Drink the cup)

Jesus, fill us with Your Spirit. Unite us in Your love. Draw us deeper into the mystery of union with You—that we may be one as You and the Father are one. Teach us to love one another with Your supernatural love. Teach us to walk in Your ways. Teach us to see our marriage not only as partnership, but as a holy vessel that carries Your glory into this world.

We receive now—with faith and joy—the blessings You have promised. Blessings of peace, healing, provision, restoration, protection, wisdom, and overflowing grace. We stand in agreement, as one, declaring that no weapon formed against us shall prosper. We break every assignment of the enemy against our lives and marriage. We release blessings over our future, over our family, and over the generations to come.

Thank You for every answered prayer, every breakthrough, every moment of grace. Help us notice, celebrate, and give thanks. Let joy fill our hearts and home.

Thank You, Jesus. Amen.

FINAL WORD

Celebration is spiritual. Joy is holy. Take time this week to rejoice in what God has done, not because everything is perfect, but because God has been faithful every step of the way.

COUPLES ACTIVITY: "VICTORY JAR"

This week, set out a jar or small box.

Each day, write down one victory, answered prayer, or moment of joy—big or small—and put it inside.

At the end of the week, sit together, read them aloud, and pray: *"Lord, thank You for all these gifts. We rejoice in You. Fill us with hope and joy as we walk into the days ahead. Amen."*

WEEK 49
PREPARING FOR JUBILEE—REST, RESTORATION, AND FREEDOM

MEDITATION SCRIPTURES

"You shall count seven sabbaths of years for yourself, seven times seven years; and the time of the seven sabbaths of years shall be to you forty-nine years. Then you shall cause the trumpet of the Jubilee to sound... And you shall consecrate the fiftieth year, and proclaim liberty throughout all the land to all its inhabitants." — Leviticus 25:8–10 (NKJV)

"Come to Me, all you who labor and are heavy laden, and I will give you rest." — Matthew 11:28 (NKJV)

"And after you have suffered a little while, the God of all grace... will Himself restore, confirm, strengthen, and establish you." — 1 Peter 5:10 (ESV)

BIBLICAL SIGNIFICANCE OF 49

In Scripture, 49 is the product of 7 x 7—seven being the number of divine completion or perfection. After 49 years, God commanded Israel to celebrate the 50th year as Jubilee:

ى debts forgiven

- و slaves set free
- و land restored
- و families reunited
- و rest given to all

Week 49, then, is not just the end of a cycle—it's preparation for release, renewal, and a fresh start.

In your marriage, this is a week to:

- و look back with gratitude
- و rest from striving
- و release old burdens, and
- و prepare your hearts for new joy and freedom

GUIDED MEDITATION ON SCRIPTURE

Sit together in quiet, maybe with soft music or candlelight.

Read the scriptures aloud slowly. Let the words *count the sabbaths… Jubilee… rest… restore… liberty* soak into your heart.

Reflect silently:

- و What burdens have we carried that we need to release?
- و Where do we long for restoration, healing, or new beginnings?
- و How can we prepare our hearts for God's "Jubilee" in our marriage—a season of freedom, joy, and blessing?

Picture God's gentle hand resting on you both, speaking, *"Well done. Rest now, and let Me carry you forward."*

QUOTE FOR TODAY

"The soul finds its Jubilee when it lets go of all but God and rests in His perfect love."

— *St. Bernard of Clairvaux*

WORD FOR THE WEEK

As you come to Week 49, pause and honor the journey. You have walked through almost a full year of seeking God, growing in love, facing struggles, celebrating joys, and deepening your bond. This week is about release—letting go of old burdens, debts, or regrets, and opening your hands to receive God's rest and renewal.

The biblical pattern shows us that after 7 x 7, God commands a pause, not just to stop working, but to restore what was broken, release what was bound, and proclaim freedom. Your marriage, too, is invited into this rhythm: to rest, forgive, heal, and celebrate all that God has done.

This is not about pretending everything is perfect. It's about trusting that God is the perfect Restorer, the One who can bring beauty from ashes, laughter from tears, and strength from weariness. Let Him declare Jubilee over your love, your home, your dreams, and your future.

This week, slow down. Breathe deep. Hold each other with tenderness. And get ready—because Jubilee is near.

PSALM TO MEDITATE ON

**"Return to your rest, my soul, for the Lord has been good to you."
— Psalm 116:7 (NIV)**

GUIDED MEDITATION ON THE PSALM

Read Psalm 116 slowly.

Ask together:

- Lord, where do we need to return to rest?
- How have You been good to us, and how can we release old weights as we prepare for new joy?

Picture yourselves laying burdens down at Jesus' feet, arms open, hearts light.

DECLARATIONS FOR THE WEEK

We declare:

- God has brought us through with faithfulness and love.
- We release old burdens, regrets, and debts into God's hands.
- Our marriage is stepping into a season of rest, joy, and renewal.
- We are preparing our hearts for Jubilee—a season of freedom and fresh beginnings.
- God's goodness carries us forward in peace.

COMMUNION PRAYER

(Prepare bread (or a cracker) and a small cup of juice. Together, hold the bread and pray).

Lord Jesus Christ, we come before You now, humbled and grateful. You are the Bread of Life, the true Manna from heaven. You gave Your body to be broken for us, that we might be made whole—spirit, soul, and body. You poured out Your blood as the cup of the new covenant, that we might be cleansed, forgiven, and reconciled to God.

We pause to remember Your sacrifice. We remember Your wounds, Your love, Your victory. We remember that You carried our sickness, our grief, our sins, and our shame upon Yourself at the cross (see Isaiah 53:4–5). You conquered death, hell, and the grave, and You rose again, so that we might share in Your life.

We confess, Lord, that we need You. We bring before You every place in our lives and marriage where we are weak, divided, hurting, or burdened. We ask for Your forgiveness for where we have spoken in anger, withheld love, carried resentment, or failed to honor one another. Wash us clean, Jesus—in Your mercy, cover us with Your righteousness.

As we eat this bread, we receive Your healing. Heal our hearts where they are wounded. Heal our minds where they are anxious or tormented. Heal our bodies where they are sick or weak. Heal our marriage where it has been strained or broken. Let the same power that raised You from the dead now flow through us. Jesus, You are our Jubilee—You forgive our debts, free our hearts, and restore our lives.

As we eat this bread, we remember Your body—given so we could rest in grace.

(Eat the bread)

As we drink this cup, we renew our covenant with You and with each other. We declare that we are Yours, and You are ours. We belong to You—as individuals and as a couple. Strengthen the bond between us. Let our love be patient, kind, humble, and enduring. Let forgiveness flow freely in our home. Let Your peace reign over our household. Jesus, thank You for Your blood, poured out for forgiveness and new life. As we drink this cup, we receive Your blood—poured out to release us into freedom and joy.

(Drink the cup)

Jesus, fill us with Your Spirit. Unite us in Your love. Draw us deeper into the mystery of union with You—that we may be one as You and the Father are one. Teach us to love one another with Your supernatural love. Teach us to walk in Your ways. Teach us to see our marriage not only as partnership, but as a holy vessel that carries Your glory into this world.

We receive now—with faith and joy—the blessings You have promised. Blessings of peace, healing, provision, restoration, protection, wisdom, and overflowing grace. We stand in agreement, as one, declaring that no weapon formed against us shall prosper. We break every assignment of the enemy against our lives and marriage.

We release blessings over our future, over our family, and over the generations to come.

We lay down all striving, all control, all weariness. We enter Your rest and prepare our hearts for a new season of blessing.

Thank You, Jesus. Amen.

FINAL WORD

Week 49 is a sacred pause—a chance to rest, remember, and release. Let it prepare you for the joyful, freeing, love-filled Jubilee God has waiting for you.

COUPLES ACTIVITY: "RELEASE AND RECEIVE"

This week, set aside time to:

- Each write down one burden, regret, or old wound you want to release.
- Pray together, giving these to God.
- Tear up or burn the paper as a symbol of release.
- Then, each name one blessing or hope you want to receive in the new season.

Pray: *"Lord, we release the old and receive the new. Thank You for carrying us and preparing us for freedom, joy, and Jubilee. Amen."*

WEEK 50
JUBILEE—ENTERING GOD'S FREEDOM, JOY, AND RENEWAL

MEDITATION SCRIPTURES

"Consecrate the fiftieth year and proclaim liberty throughout the land to all its inhabitants. It shall be a Jubilee for you." — Leviticus 25:10 (NIV)

"So if the Son sets you free, you will be free indeed." — John 8:36 (NIV)

"You crown the year with Your goodness, and Your paths drip with abundance." — Psalm 65:11 (NKJV)

BIBLICAL MEANING OF JUBILEE (50TH YEAR)

In the Bible, Jubilee was celebrated every 50th year:

- debts forgiven
- slaves set free
- land restored
- families reunited
- rest given to the land and the people

It was a God-ordained reset—not earned, but gifted—overflowing with mercy, restoration, and joyful celebration.

For your marriage, Week 50 marks a spiritual Jubilee:

- ﻭ a time to forgive and release
- ﻭ to celebrate what God has done
- ﻭ to receive fresh joy
- ﻭ to declare freedom and blessing over your love and your home.

GUIDED MEDITATION ON SCRIPTURE

Sit together quietly, maybe with soft worship music or candlelight.

Read the scriptures aloud slowly. Let the words *consecrate... proclaim liberty... free indeed... crown the year with goodness... abundance* fill your hearts.

Reflect silently:

- ﻭ Where have we seen God's freedom at work in our marriage this year?
- ﻭ What burdens or old patterns do we need to release as we step into Jubilee?
- ﻭ What blessings, dreams, or new joys are we ready to receive together?

Imagine God smiling over you, His hands open wide, saying, *"Welcome into Jubilee, My beloved ones."*

QUOTE FOR TODAY

"The soul sings in its Jubilee when it is free to love God without fear, without burden, and without end."

— *St. John of the Cross*

WORD FOR THE WEEK

This is your Jubilee. You have walked through joys, struggles, prayers, healing, growth, and love. And now God invites you to celebrate not just where you've been, but where He's taking you next.

Jubilee is a time of release—to let go of old debts, grudges, fears, or regrets. It's a time of restoration—to reclaim dreams, tenderness, laughter, and unity. And it's a time of rest—to pause, breathe, and simply enjoy the gift of each other and God's presence.

God is not asking you to "arrive" at perfection. He's inviting you to step into freedom—the freedom of being deeply loved, fully forgiven, and joyfully blessed. As a couple, this means walking forward lighter, freer, more open to each other and to Him.

This week, rejoice. Celebrate. Dance. Laugh. Pray. Bless. Let God crown your year—and your marriage—with goodness and abundance.

PSALM TO MEDITATE ON

"The Lord has done great things for us, and we are filled with joy." — Psalm 126:3 (NIV)

GUIDED MEDITATION ON THE PSALM

Read Psalm 126:3 aloud, maybe more than once.

Ask together:

- ی Lord, what are the "great things" You have done for us this year?
- ی How can we thank You and rejoice fully in this Jubilee season?

Picture yourselves lifting your faces to heaven, hearts full of gratitude and joy.

DECLARATIONS FOR THE WEEK

We declare:

- ی We are forgiven, free, and deeply loved.
- ی We step into a season of joy, restoration, and blessing.
- ی We release every old weight and receive fresh grace.
- ی Our marriage is crowned with God's goodness and abundance.
- ی We walk forward in love, freedom, and joyful expectation.

COMMUNION PRAYER

**(Prepare bread (or a cracker) and a small cup of juice.
Together, hold the bread and pray).**

Lord Jesus Christ, we come before You now, humbled and grateful. You are the Bread of Life, the true Manna from heaven. You gave Your body to be broken for us, that we might be made whole—spirit, soul, and body. You poured out Your blood as the cup of the new covenant, that we might be cleansed, forgiven, and reconciled to God.

We pause to remember Your sacrifice. We remember Your wounds, Your love, Your victory. We remember that You carried our sickness, our grief, our sins, and our shame upon Yourself at the cross (see Isaiah 53:4–5). You conquered death, hell, and the grave, and You rose again, so that we might share in Your life.

We confess, Lord, that we need You. We bring before You every place in our lives and marriage where we are weak, divided, hurting, or burdened. We ask for Your forgiveness for where we have spoken in anger, withheld love, carried resentment, or failed to honor one another. Wash us clean, Jesus—in Your mercy, cover us with Your righteousness.

As we eat this bread, we receive Your healing. Heal our hearts where they are wounded. Heal our minds where they are anxious or tormented. Heal our bodies where they are sick or weak. Heal our marriage where it has been strained or broken. Let the same power that raised You from the dead now flow through us. Jesus, You are our Jubilee—You paid every debt, freed every captive, and opened the way to joy and rest. As we eat this bread, we remember Your body—given to break every chain.

(Eat the bread)

As we drink this cup, we renew our covenant with You and with each other. We declare that we are Yours, and You are ours. We belong to You—as individuals and as a couple. Strengthen the bond between us. Let our love be patient, kind, humble, and enduring. Let forgiveness flow freely in our home. Let Your peace reign over our household. Jesus, thank You for Your blood, poured out for forgiveness and new life. As we drink this cup, we receive Your blood—poured out to cover us with mercy and love.

(Drink the cup)

Jesus, fill us with Your Spirit. Unite us in Your love. Draw us deeper into the mystery of union with You—that we may be one as You and the Father are one. Teach us to love one another with Your supernatural love. Teach us to walk in Your ways. Teach us to see our marriage not only as partnership, but as a holy vessel that carries Your glory into this world.

We receive now—with faith and joy—the blessings You have promised. Blessings of peace, healing, provision, restoration, protection, wisdom, and overflowing grace. We stand in agreement, as one, declaring that no weapon formed against us shall prosper. We break every assignment of the enemy against our lives and marriage.

We release blessings over our future, over our family, and over the generations to come.

We receive Your Jubilee over our lives, our marriage, and our future. We step into this new season with open hands, open hearts, and open joy.

Thank You, Jesus. Amen.

FINAL WORD

Jubilee is God's declaration over you: *"You are free. You are blessed. You are Mine."* Step forward together, laughing, loving, and rejoicing because the best is yet to come.

COUPLES ACTIVITY: "THE JUBILEE CELEBRATION"

Set aside special time this week to:

- ﻼ Celebrate! Cook a special meal, go for a meaningful walk, dance in the living room, or share communion together.

- ﻼ Pray a blessing over each other, aloud: *"I bless you with joy, peace, love, and freedom. May God fill you with His abundance in this new season."*

- ﻼ Write down or speak out three dreams or hopes you want to carry into your next chapter.

JUBILEE BLESSING OVER OUR MARRIAGE

Heavenly Father,

We stand here at the edge of Jubilee, not by our own strength, but by Your mercy, not because we have been perfect, but because You are faithful. Thank You for bringing us through these weeks of devotion, for walking with us through joys, struggles, prayers, and growth. Thank You for being the restorer of our souls, the healer of our hearts, and the builder of our love.

And now, Lord, we speak Your Jubilee blessing over our marriage. We release old burdens, old debts, old wounds. We forgive, and we ask to be forgiven. We let go of the things that weighed us down, and we lift our eyes to You—the God of fresh beginnings.

We bless our home to be a place of peace and joy. We bless our love to grow deeper, kinder, and freer. We bless our future to overflow with hope, dreams, laughter, and purpose. We bless our bodies to be strong, our minds to be renewed, and our spirits to walk in freedom.

In the name of Jesus, we proclaim:

- ۍ This is a new season.
- ۍ This is a season of rest, release, and restoration.

ﺱ This is a season of freedom, joy, and abundance.

ﺱ This is our Jubilee.

Thank You, Lord, that we are Yours, and You are ours, forever. In Jesus' name. Amen.

After praying this, you may want to exchange a simple physical symbol —

ﺱ a touch on the forehead

ﺱ a light kiss on the forehead or hands

ﺱ or even a small gift or written note —

to seal this moment with love and tenderness.

WEEK 51
LEAVING A LEGACY—SOWING SEEDS FOR GENERATIONS

MEDITATION SCRIPTURES

"The righteous man walks in his integrity; his children are blessed after him." — Proverbs 20:7 (NKJV)

"One generation shall praise Your works to another, and shall declare Your mighty acts." — Psalm 145:4 (NKJV)

"Let your light so shine before men, that they may see your good works and glorify your Father in heaven." — Matthew 5:16 (NKJV)

GUIDED MEDITATION ON SCRIPTURE

Sit together in quiet, maybe holding hands or sitting close.

Read the scriptures aloud slowly. Let the words *integrity… blessed after him… one generation… let your light shine* settle in your hearts.

Reflect silently:

ა What kind of legacy are we building in our marriage—in love, faith, forgiveness, generosity, and service?

- How are we impacting the lives of those closest to us—family, friends, community?
- What seeds do we want to plant now that will bear fruit for years, even beyond us?

Picture your marriage as a tree, its roots deep, its branches wide, offering shade, fruit, and beauty to those around you.

QUOTE FOR TODAY

"The soul that burns with love cannot keep it to itself; it must pass the flame, that the world may be warmed."

— *St. Catherine of Siena*

WORD FOR THE WEEK

Marriage is never just about two people.

The love, faith, forgiveness, and choices you live out together ripple outward—shaping children, encouraging friends, blessing your community, and pointing others toward God.

Your legacy is not measured in wealth or achievements, but in the seeds you sow:

- A word of encouragement here.
- A choice to forgive there.
- A family tradition of prayer, kindness, or service.
- A life that says, *"Our love is rooted in something greater."*

This week is an invitation to reflect, not in pressure, but in purpose.

What story is your marriage telling? What are you passing on—through your words, your choices, your example? Remember, you don't have to be perfect to leave a beautiful legacy. You simply have to keep showing up, loving, repenting, forgiving, and shining God's light.

PSALM TO MEDITATE ON

"May the Lord give you increase, you and your children. May you be blessed by the Lord, who made heaven and earth." — Psalm 115:14–15 (ESV)

GUIDED MEDITATION ON THE PSALM

Read Psalm 115:14-15 slowly, perhaps with hands open.

Ask together:

- Lord, what blessings have You poured into our marriage that we want to pass on?
- How can we pray for, bless, or encourage the next generation this week?

Picture God's hands open over you, pouring blessing, so you can pour out to others.

DECLARATIONS FOR THE WEEK

We declare:

- ى Our marriage is a light, a testimony, and a blessing to others.
- ى We sow seeds of love, faith, hope, and kindness.
- ى God increases the work of our hands and blesses our home.
- ى We will leave a legacy of grace and truth for future generations.
- ى We walk in purpose, knowing our lives matter in God's kingdom.

COMMUNION PRAYER

(Prepare bread (or a cracker) and a small cup of juice. Together, hold the bread and pray).

Lord Jesus Christ, we come before You now, humbled and grateful. You are the Bread of Life, the true Manna from heaven. You gave Your body to be broken for us, that we might be made whole—spirit, soul, and body. You poured out Your blood as the cup of the new covenant, that we might be cleansed, forgiven, and reconciled to God.

We pause to remember Your sacrifice. We remember Your wounds, Your love, Your victory. We remember that You carried our sickness, our grief, our sins, and our shame upon Yourself at the cross (see Isaiah 53:4–5). You conquered death, hell, and the grave, and You rose again, so that we might share in Your life.

We confess, Lord, that we need You. We bring before You every place in our lives and marriage where we are weak, divided, hurting, or burdened. We ask for Your forgiveness for where we have spoken in anger, withheld love, carried resentment, or failed to honor one another. Wash us clean, Jesus—in Your mercy, cover us with Your righteousness.

As we eat this bread, we receive Your healing. Heal our hearts where they are wounded. Heal our minds where they are anxious or tormented. Heal our bodies where they are sick or weak. Heal our marriage where it has been strained or broken. Let the same power that raised You from the dead now flow through us. Jesus, You are the vine, and we are the branches. In You, we bear fruit that will last—fruit of love, peace, and joy for others. As we eat this bread, we remember Your body—broken to bring us into God's family.

(Eat the bread)

As we drink this cup, we renew our covenant with You and with each other. We declare that we are Yours, and You are ours. We belong to You—as individuals and as a couple. Strengthen the bond between us. Let our love be patient, kind, humble, and enduring. Let forgiveness flow freely in our home. Let Your peace reign over our household. Jesus, thank You for Your blood, poured out for forgiveness and new life. As we drink this cup, we receive Your blood—poured out to give us eternal hope.

(Drink the cup)

Jesus, fill us with Your Spirit. Unite us in Your love. Draw us deeper into the mystery of union with You—that we may be one as You and the Father are one. Teach us to love one another with Your supernatural love. Teach us to walk in Your ways. Teach us to see our marriage not only as partnership, but as a holy vessel that carries Your glory into this world.

We receive now—with faith and joy—the blessings You have promised. Blessings of peace, healing, provision, restoration, protection, wisdom, and overflowing grace. We stand in agreement, as one, declaring that no weapon formed against us shall prosper. We break every assignment of the enemy against our lives and marriage. We release blessings over our future, over our family, and over the generations to come.

Help us, Lord, to live and love in a way that leaves a mark of Your goodness. Let our marriage be a living witness to Your grace. Let our legacy bring You glory.

Thank You, Jesus. Amen.

FINAL WORD

Legacy is not about perfection—it's about faithfulness.

This week, walk with the quiet joy of knowing that your love matters, your story matters, and God is using you to shape lives beyond your own.

COUPLES ACTIVITY: "BLESSING THE NEXT GENERATION"

Set aside time this week to:

- ᦂ Pray for your children, grandchildren, nieces/nephews, godchildren, or young couples you know.
- ᦂ Write a letter, note, or prayer of blessing to someone from the next generation.
- ᦂ **Talk together:** What is one family tradition or value we want to intentionally pass on?

Pray together: *"Lord, let our love point others to You. May those who come after us be blessed, strengthened, and inspired by the seeds we plant today. Amen."*

WEEK 52
COMMISSIONED IN LOVE—A
MARRIAGE FOR GOD'S GLORY

MEDITATION SCRIPTURES

"Now to Him who is able to do immeasurably more than all we ask or imagine, according to His power that is at work within us, to Him be glory in the church and in Christ Jesus throughout all generations, forever and ever! Amen." — Ephesians 3:20–21 (NIV)

"As for me and my house, we will serve the Lord." — Joshua 24:15 (NKJV)

"The Lord bless you and keep you; the Lord make His face shine upon you and be gracious to you; the Lord lift up His countenance upon you, and give you peace." — Numbers 6:24–26 (NKJV)

GUIDED MEDITATION ON SCRIPTURE

Sit together quietly, maybe in candlelight or holding hands.

Read the scriptures aloud slowly. Let the words *immeasurably more… His power… glory… serve the Lord… bless and keep you* echo deep into your hearts.

Reflect silently:

- ৬ What has God done in us, for us, and through us this year?
- ৬ What are we thankful for as we close this devotional journey?
- ৬ How is God calling us forward—as a couple, as a family, as His servants?

Imagine God smiling over you, hands stretched in blessing, saying: *"Well done. Keep walking with Me."*

QUOTE FOR TODAY

"Love has no end; it grows into eternity. All we do for love's sake will never be lost."

— *St. Teresa of Ávila*

WORD FOR THE WEEK

You have completed a full year of walking intentionally, prayerfully, and lovingly together. Week after week, you've pressed into God's heart, faced joys and struggles, laughed and wept, healed and grown. This is holy ground.

But this is not the end—it's the beginning.
You are not just a couple who survived 52 weeks of devotions; you are a couple commissioned in love, marked by God's faithfulness, equipped with His truth, and sent into the world to shine His glory.

Your marriage is now a living testimony—not of perfection, but of perseverance, grace, and transformation.

You are called to carry His love into your home, your church, your community, your friendships, and wherever He leads next.

So pause. Celebrate. Give thanks. And then rise up—ready to serve, to love, to give, and to walk forward into the "immeasurably more" God has for you.

PSALM TO MEDITATE ON

"Let everything that has breath praise the Lord. Praise the Lord!"
— Psalm 150:6 (NKJV)

GUIDED MEDITATION ON THE PSALM

Read Psalm 150:6 aloud, maybe even joyfully or with a little smile.

Ask together:

- Lord, how can we keep praising You in our everyday lives?
- What is one act of service, love, or joy we can commit to as a couple going forward?

Picture your home filled with praise—through laughter, kindness, worship, and love.

DECLARATIONS FOR THE WEEK

We declare:

- ‫ God has been faithful to us through every season.
- ‫ Our marriage belongs to God—for His glory and purpose.
- ‫ We will serve the Lord with joy, love, and faithfulness.
- ‫ We carry God's blessing into our future and into the lives we touch.
- ‫ We are commissioned as a couple, walking forward in love and power.

COMMUNION PRAYER

(Prepare bread (or a cracker) and a small cup of juice. Together, hold the bread and pray).

Lord Jesus Christ, we come before You now, humbled and grateful. You are the Bread of Life, the true Manna from heaven. You gave Your body to be broken for us, that we might be made whole—spirit, soul, and body. You poured out Your blood as the cup of the new covenant, that we might be cleansed, forgiven, and reconciled to God.

We pause to remember Your sacrifice. We remember Your wounds, Your love, Your victory. We remember that You carried our sickness, our grief, our sins, and our shame upon Yourself at the cross (see Isaiah 53:4–5). You conquered death, hell, and the grave, and You rose again, so that we might share in Your life.

We confess, Lord, that we need You. We bring before You every place in our lives and marriage where we are weak, divided, hurting, or burdened. We ask for Your forgiveness for where we have spoken in anger, withheld love, carried resentment, or failed to honor one another. Wash us clean, Jesus—in Your mercy, cover us with Your righteousness.

As we eat this bread, we receive Your healing. Heal our hearts where they are wounded. Heal our minds where they are anxious or tormented. Heal our bodies where they are sick or weak. Heal our marriage where it has been strained or broken. Let the same power that raised You from the dead now flow through us. Jesus, You have been our Rock, our Healer, our Joy, and our Savior. You have walked with us through 52 weeks of seeking, growing, and loving. As we eat this bread, we remember Your body—sustaining us through every trial.

(Eat the bread)

As we drink this cup, we renew our covenant with You and with each other. We declare that we are Yours, and You are ours. We belong to You—as individuals and as a couple. Strengthen the bond between us. Let our love be patient, kind, humble, and enduring. Let forgiveness flow freely in our home. Let Your peace reign over our household. Jesus, thank You for Your blood, poured out for forgiveness and new life. As we drink this cup, we receive Your blood—covering us with forgiveness, hope, and power.

(Drink the cup)

Jesus, fill us with Your Spirit. Unite us in Your love. Draw us deeper into the mystery of union with You—that we may be one as You and the Father are one. Teach us to love one another with Your supernatural love. Teach us to walk in Your ways. Teach us to see our marriage not only as partnership, but as a holy vessel that carries Your glory into this world.

We receive now—with faith and joy—the blessings You have promised. Blessings of peace, healing, provision, restoration, protection, wisdom, and overflowing grace. We stand in agreement, as one, declaring that no weapon formed against us shall prosper. We break every assignment of the enemy against our lives and marriage. We release blessings over our future, over our family, and over the generations to come.

We consecrate our marriage to You, Lord. We say: as for us, we will serve You. Send us. Use us. Shine through us. Let our love glorify You, today and always.

Thank You, Jesus. Amen.

FINAL WORD

You are a love story written by God—not just for yourselves, but for the world. Carry this light forward, knowing He is not finished with you—the best is yet to come.

COUPLES ACTIVITY: "COVENANT RENEWAL"

This week, consider doing a simple renewal ceremony:

- ও Write or speak short vows of love, faithfulness, and purpose to each other.
- ও Pray a blessing over your future: *"Lord, thank You for this love. Use us for Your glory. Keep us close, keep us faithful, keep us shining for You. Amen."*
- ও Celebrate with a special dinner, a walk, or a symbolic act (such as lighting a candle, exchanging small tokens, or taking communion).

FINAL AUTHOR'S BLESSING

Beloved couples,

As you close these 52 weeks, I want to bless you, not only as an author, but as a fellow pilgrim on the journey of love, faith, and marriage.

I bless your hearts to stay soft toward God and toward each other. I bless your hands to keep reaching for each other, even on the hard days. I bless your home to be filled with laughter, honesty, forgiveness, and grace. I bless your prayers to be bold, your service to be joyful, and your love to be strong. I bless your marriage to be a light—in your family, your church, your community, and the world.

May you walk forward knowing you are deeply loved, chosen, and equipped. The God who brought you this far is not finished with you—the best is yet to come. Walk in His blessing. Walk in His joy. Walk in His power.

With love, prayers, and honor,
Cleveland Orville McLeish, MTS

CLOSING LETTER TO THE READER

Dear friends,

Thank you.

Thank you for opening these pages, for showing up each week, for seeking God together in your marriage, and for pressing into His presence with honesty and courage.

You have not walked this journey alone. God has been with you—in the quiet moments, in the tears and laughter, in the prayers whispered at night, and in the little victories no one else saw.

This devotional was never about perfect performance. It was always about learning to walk together toward God, again and again, day by day, hand in hand.

As you step beyond these pages, carry this truth with you: **Your love matters. Your marriage matters.** Not because it is flawless, but because it is His. You are part of His great story of redemption, love, and grace in the world.

Keep going. Keep growing. Keep shining. And never forget—you are not just husband and wife; you are a team, a testimony, and a light.

MARRIAGE COMMISSIONING PRAYER

Heavenly Father,

We stand before You today with grateful hearts. Thank You for carrying this couple through 52 weeks of devotion, growth, and love. Thank You for being their healer, provider, teacher, and friend.

And now, Lord, we commission them in Your name. We commission them to love—with patience, tenderness, forgiveness, and joy. We commission them to serve—each other, their family, their church, and their world. We commission them to pray—boldly, faithfully, expectantly. We commission them to shine—as a light of Your presence and love wherever they go.

We declare that their marriage is Yours, their home is blessed, their future is secure in Your hands.

Holy Spirit, fill them afresh. Anoint their love. Strengthen their hearts. Renew their dreams. Multiply their fruit. And let their lives bring You glory, now and always.

In Jesus' mighty name we pray. Amen.

"Now to him who is able to do far more abundantly than all that we ask or think, according to the power at work within us, to him be glory in the church and in Christ Jesus throughout all generations, forever and ever. Amen." — Ephesians 3:20–21 (ESV)

DECLARATION

We declare this marriage to be blessed, strengthened, and commissioned for God's glory.

May you walk forward in love, hope, joy, and the fullness of God's purpose—today and always.

FINAL BENEDICTION

"The Lord bless you and keep you; the Lord make his face to shine upon you and be gracious to you; the Lord lift up his countenance upon you and give you peace." — Numbers 6:24–26 (ESV)

www.ingramcontent.com/pod-product-compliance
Lightning Source LLC
Chambersburg PA
CBHW071702120626
46550CB00001B/77

9 781965 635681